Diary of a Dean

Herbert I. London

Hamilton Books
A member of
The Rowman & Littlefield Publishing Group
Lanham • Boulder • New York • Toronto • Plymouth, UK

Copyright © 2010 by
Hamilton Books
4501 Forbes Boulevard
Suite 200
Lanham, Maryland 20706
Hamilton Books Acquisitions Department (301) 459-3366

Estover Road
Plymouth PL6 7PY
United Kingdom

All rights reserved
Printed in the United States of America
British Library Cataloging in Publication Information Available

Library of Congress Control Number: 2010926908
ISBN 978-0-7618-5171-4 (paperback : alk. paper)
eISBN 978-0-7618-5172-1

∞™ The paper used in this publication meets the minimum
requirements of American National Standard for Information
Sciences—Permanence of Paper for Printed Library Materials,
ANSI Z39.48—1992

Contents

Preface	v
Introduction	vii
1 Thinking about America from Down Under	1
2 How a Commencement Changed My Life	7
3 Running to Class	13
4 Underground Notes from a Campus Ombudsman	17
5 What a Dean Learns from His Mother	29
6 What Really Matters	37
7 Letter to a Student	41
8 The Zeitgeist Rings My Home Number	45
9 Challenging the Academic Orthodoxy	51
10 The Tenure Trap	57
11 Academic Freedom and Free Speech	59
12 The Hudson Institute as a University in Absentia	63
Conclusion	67

Preface

This is a brief memoir about one dimension of my professional life. Although an idiosyncratic story, it is woven through the turbulent history of university life in the late sixties and seventies, a time that left an indelible mark on higher education.

I don't purport to know more than my colleagues or suggest that I was more right than wrong in my university decisions, but I can assert I was in the eye of the hurricane blown about and occasionally battered, but still maintaining some grasp on my convictions.

My hope is that the reader will be enriched by the stories that follow, and will also digest the lessons learned. For I believe, the road to recovery in the Academy lie in the lessons implicit and sometimes explicit in the pages that follow.

HIL

Introduction

As a teenager nothing was more important to me than playing basketball. I dreamed of entering the pro ranks. I watched games on TV incessantly.

Eventually, I played in high school, made the All–New York City team and eagerly thought about b-ball in college. My dad admired a Yale basketball player who tried out for the Knicks, played the accordion and sang on the *Ed Sullivan Show*. I too sang, was given an accordion to play (my mom said you can be the whole orchestra) and had a miniature basketball placed in my crib. Hence, whether I liked it or not, my fate was sealed.

Since my dad was most impressed with Lou Rossini, the Columbia coach, I ended up on Morningside Heights. It wasn't Yale, but even Dad had to admit it was a close call. In the first year, I was in a terrible automobile accident and broke my clavicle twice in basketball scrimmages. I was persuaded a black cloud was right over my head. It was a lost year. I barely passed Dr. Farenholt's chemistry course, and I was befuddled with study, overwhelmed by my duties as a waiter in Johnson Hall and frustrated with my inability to stay uninjured.

But despite these problems, there was a transformation taking place, incremental at first and then in a torrent. It was due in large part to "C.C. Hum," the two year required courses in Contemporary Civilization and the Humanities in which I was exposed to the Greek classics, the Bible and every notable philosopher and Western thinker. The great books spoke to me; they awakened a dormant thirst for knowledge.

This quest to learn more was enhanced by William Casey's course in social theory. I read Pitirim Sorokin as if it were the Bible, memorizing passages and actually reading books that weren't on the assignment list. No, I didn't give up basketball. Having finally remained injury free, I made the starting team. Basketball was important, but my thoughts often strayed from the hardwood to dusty stacks in the Butler Library.

Although the prominent professors I was exposed to meant little to me at the time, years later I came to appreciate the books and ideas of the Van Dorens, both Mark and Charles (father and son), my advisors Sam Huntington and Daniel Bell and a young lecturer named Amitai Etzioni. Although the prevailing political sentiment leaned leftwards on campus, as did I, there was a categorical refusal to impose orthodoxies of either the left or the right. Richard Hofstadter, a Columbia professor, had published *Paranoid Style in American History* which seemed to suggest paranoia was a condition solely restricted to right-wing politics, but this had not yet registered as biased opinion.

Political correctness had not invaded the campus, although one experience I had as a research assistant seemed to suggest the seeds for left-wing allegiance had been planted. For a short time I was a research assistant for C. Wright Mills, a sociologist of some renown, who was working on a book about Fidel Castro later published as *Listen Yankee*. During the course of research I discovered that the United Fruit Company was not the exploitive, imperialistic and hated company Mills made it out to be. After presenting my findings, Mills dismissed me and the facts with a wave of his arm as if to say don't confuse me with the evidence.

Notwithstanding my encounter with Mills, the Columbia campus invited controversy. I was intoxicated by the variety of thoughtful opinion. Although I was certainly not a brilliant student, I couldn't wait to taste the delectable morsels of knowledge in every class. In fact, by my junior year I had abandoned pre-med studies (a significant emotional blow for my parents) and became enchanted with the idea of an academic career.

The subsequent years flew by. My reading became intense. After a stint teaching in a high school for spoiled kids, I decided to enroll in a PhD program at NYU. New York University was thought of by snobbish Columbians as that marginal university for commuters downtown at Washington Square. I discovered something else. Perhaps it was the Avis in New York, but NYU strived to be at least as prestigious as Columbia and was far more open to ideas than its uptown counterpart.

Since I was intent on obtaining my "union card" as soon as possible, I worked feverishly on the completion of course requirements and my dissertation. Receiving the degree meant a great deal to me and my folks. I wasn't the doctor they had in mind, but I was a doctor. Having completed my degree by writing about nativism in New York, I was interested in pursing anti-immigration legislation outside the U.S. At the time Australia had a White Australia Policy, a policy designed to maintain an ostensibly British culture in a sea of Asians. By 1966 when Japan became Australia's leading trading partner, "White Australia" became an embarrassment. The Australian government engaged in curious twists and turns to maintain the policy and maintain its new trading ties, including calling Japanese caucasians for the purpose of trade. But the policy wasn't sustainable.

It seemed to me it was a great time to study the forces liberalizing the policy. After applying for and receiving a Fulbright fellowship, I went to the Australian National University in Canberra where I worked on a major study of Australian immigration policy. This resulted in my first scholarly book, *Non-White Immigration and The White Australian Policy*. It also led to my first academic appointment at NYU.

While my teaching experience was limited, I taught with great enthusiasm. My goal was to excite students about ideas the way I was turned on during my undergraduate years at Columbia. But I didn't appreciate the *zeitgeist*. It was the late sixties. The war in Vietnam was heating up, Robert Kennedy had been assassinated, Gene McCarthy seemed to capture the acceptance of the young, Martin Luther King was murdered. The world was being turned topsy-turvy. This generation of students wanted action. Even those who were normally contemplative were caught up in the wave of ideological sentiment. Most students wanted to change the society, albeit the words and deeds of social transformation did not translate into a strategic vision. These were the children of privilege who, filled with innocence and idealism, thought their enthusiasm was sufficient to alter the culture. And to some degree they were right. Traditions toppled like a house of cards, and the university representing those traditions was most vulnerable.

One day as I passed Waverly Place on my way to class, I saw graffito on a wall that seemed to embody the spirit in this youthful culture. It read, "Make them teach you only what to learn." I was part of "them" and if you accepted the sentiment in this sentence the core curriculum was an unjust attempt to transmit the justification for the existing power structure. Here was democratization with a vengeance.

My education about the culture and Woodstock generation was about to begin. From 1967 to 1973 spring didn't merely bring blossoms to Washington Square Park, it brought demonstrations. An explosion on nearby 11th Street pointed to an inherent violence in the radical student movements. One of those involved in this violence, Kathy Boudin was the daughter of an NYU faculty member. The violence had come right to my doorstep. Classes were routinely suspended during this period. Although it is something of an exaggeration, many of the students graduating from universities during this period majored in dope smoking and demonstrations.

This was the period that profoundly influenced my view of the Academy. I realized that the university was changing and, from my perspective, the change wasn't salutary.

Chapter One

Thinking about America from Down Under

Having completed my dissertation on a political aspect of the American nativist movement, I had a desire to compare the experience in the 19th century with contemporary examples.

In effect, I wanted to do a comparative analysis of immigration policies that would enable me to test hypotheses I had explored in one culture and, at the same time, give me an excuse for going abroad, a kind of reward for a year of tedious doctoral research. So, with my recently obtained degree in hand, I applied for a Fulbright grant to Australia. It was the first test of the degree's utility, and it passed with flying colors. In August of 1966, I left for the land Down Under.

If there is one country on the globe that bears comparison with the United States, it is Australia. While other nations decry American values and policies, Australians unashamedly embrace them. When I asked an average Australian what he expected from life, he didn't hesitate to reply: "V.B., tele, and footy." (That's Australian slang or "strine" for Victorian Bitter beer, television, and Australian rules football.) Australians value their comfort and their relatively tranquil lifestyle. They can be insufferably complacent and charmingly innocent. Despite the radical views of college-age youth, who are amenable to the idealism of the left and are sometimes vigorously anti-American, or those views held by patricians, who are self-consciously British and characterize Americans as parvenus, the population is overwhelmingly pro-American.

After a rather tedious orientation session at the university, I was introduced to my advisor. He was a tall man who looked like Walter Pidgeon and talked like Terry Thomas. He radiated all the warmth of Count Dracula. Despite their bravado, Australians are generally uncomfortable in groups outside of a pub. For almost two weeks I went to my assigned office without talking to anyone. Even during tea breaks (at 10:30 AM and 3:30 PM), I sipped my tea in complete isolation. Apparently, no one thought it the least bit odd that the newest member of the politics department sat alone. This condition remained unaltered for almost a month. It also prevailed in the rather stodgy place where I resided, a dormitory normally reserved for visiting dignitaries. It had common tables, but I never had any difficulty eating my meals in utter silence. In fact, the only words I ever spoke were at one of my infrequent invitations to "high table," a British institution that is a fading relic of Commonwealth ties.

It was during an afternoon tea break that my silence finally ended. An athletic-looking fellow was trying to elicit interest in a softball game. I would barely contain myself. "Hey, you! I'd love to play." Heads turned as half the people in the room wondered where I had found my tongue. In no time my competitive zeal was displayed. I helped to organize a league, explained the rules and, not coincidentally, became the main interpreter of the rules. If any single fact underscored the difference between the Aussies and myself, it was a softball game.

Like Etonians, these men came dressed in whites. They didn't pitch, they bowled. And if, perchance, one of their "mites" got a hit, they applauded politely and said "good shew." For an old stickball player, the proprieties were odd and annoying. I screamed at the opposing pitcher, cursed when someone on my team made an error, and came close to punching the umpire in a dispute over a bad call. I was a complete enigma to the Australians, a curiosity that was at once brash and resourceful. It seemed extremely odd that this normally laconic American should get so worked up over a modified cricket game.

My habits were undoubtedly strange, but I found Australian post-game habits very natural—excessively natural. A beer after a long afternoon at play is often what a sport is all about. But Aussies drink until taking another sip without barfing becomes an excruciating ordeal. The usual pub is, understandably, completely tiled, and looks like a men's room with a podium. When someone does vomit, which is not at all unusual, a barmaid gets a hose and washes the wall down; for this service, she receives about as much attention as someone who sneezes on a New York subway platform.

It is a matter of pride that everyone have a chance to "shout" (order and pay for the drinks) for everyone in the group. If the group includes ten men, the number on a softball team, ten pints of beer will be consumed in a matter of two or three hours. After a session at the pub I invariably crawled back to my room too sloshed to find my bed, yet still sober enough to be amazed at the capacity of the average Australian for beer.

One morning, I had an appointment to see the leader of the opposition party in the House of Representatives. It was 10:00 AM, but this gentleman—a W.

C. Fields look-a-like—was already putting away glasses of Johnnie Walker Black Label. When I inquired about his country's immigration policy, he burped and said, "Damn good." I wasn't sure whether he was referring to the booze or the policy. On another occasion I invited a representative to dinner at the dormitory, a fellow who had been in the House for twenty-eight consecutive years. It was the only meal I have ever drunk in my life. We started with sherry, had claret between mouthfuls of steak, had cognac after dinner, and finished with some serious beer drinking. I found that my modest stipend barely covered my liquor bills. I also discovered that even when these meals were arranged for research purposes, I could never recall what was said.

Life for the Australian academic can be absolutely idyllic. There is simply no pressure: the "publish or perish" chant has not yet reached their shores. Aside from a weekly seminar, academics at the Australian National University could only be seen in the tea room. Presumably, they were busy at work on research that would expand the frontiers of knowledge. On occasion, though, I spied these alleged researchers snoozing behind open newspapers. The combination of free time, little pressure and surrounding that would make the Palm Springs set envious does not inspire industry. With my New York orientation, pressure was self-imposed; I stood out like a rate-buster in a construction union.

As one might expect, discussions of Australian policies were on the scheduled agenda at the infrequent seminars that constituted the only noticeable pressure on the resident academics. Invariably, the exchanges seemed to center upon Vietnam—the sole preoccupation of almost everyone in 1967—even among otherwise complacent Australian professors. Having been an antiwar advocate since 1963—when my regular reading of I. F. Stone began – or before I learned about his ties to the Soviet Union – these discussions were usually interesting, so interesting, in fact, that I was probably the only American of my age to be converted from antiwar advocate to an equivocal prowar defender in the period from 1965 to 1967. I continued to equivocate because, as a New York liberal (before I was mugged by reality), I just couldn't be prowar. Australians can present a very convincing case for balance-of-power theories that, to most American seem like scribbles on Herman Kahn's blackboard. Australia almost went to war with Indonesia in the early sixties, and the people still possess vivid recollections of the Japanese invasion of Darwin in 1942. It is interesting to note, too, that the distance between Darwin and Saigon is less than the distance between Sydney and Darwin, a fact that was used as a justification for Australia's interest in Asian affairs. Nonetheless, from an early-sixties perspective it became easy for me to understand why former Prime Minister Robert Menzies could prevail upon the United States to get involved in Southeast Asia through the SEATO Treaty.

Australia was hardly one of those dominoes discussed at length by Dulles and Eisenhower, but it had good historical reasons for fearing the worst. For narrow-minded peaceniks of the sixties, only "presentism" served as a guide for policy decisions. Having been a former peacenik, I understood the syndrome; moreover, I also came to understand what foreign policy position the United States had been trying to evolve.

It must seem strange that a kid from Brooklyn would be moving directly against the historical current. But American power can appear to be quite different when viewed from a relatively weak state possessing modest defense capabilities. Having been taught a foreign policy view predicated on an aversion to brinkmanship and isolationism, it wasn't too difficult for me to accept the idea of America's international role in a "conventional war." What was difficult, however, was retaining my liberal credentials when all of my so-called liberal friends were making sounds that were unmistakably isolationist.

What this analysis suggests is that the America one sees from the other side of the world is not so evil as critics would have us believe. Notwithstanding the view of Susan Sontag, the world would not be better off if America incinerated itself. While left-wing critics deride our culture as patently vapid, Australians wait patiently for hours to see a revival of Gone with the Wind. While antiwar critics denounced American participation in "an unnecessary and shameful war," there were people in the South Pacific who genuinely appreciated our war efforts. While social theorists and others decry the national tendency toward conformity, this land still offers more options for self-expression then presently exist in Australia. Why else would all those Australian actors and musicians come here?

Despite the stark beauty of the land and my growing fondness for many Aussies, I couldn't wait to leave the country. Australians provincialism was just too taxing after Greenwich Village. I'll never forget the time I went to see Mai Zetterling's Night Games in Melbourne, only to sit through a thirty-five-minute version of the two-hour film that had been thoroughly sliced and spliced by the state censor. Similarly, when I ordered books from abroad, I received a note instructing me to pick them up at a customs' office, a rather unusual practice. When I inquired about my property, the customs officer asked if I were importing lewd literature for public distribution. You see, among the books I had ordered was a copy of Alain Resnais's screenplay for Hiroshima Mon Amour; the book included film stills, one of which showed a nude couple in bed.

It is also true that I missed being in America. There is nothing in Australia that can duplicate the sights and sounds of Greenwich Village. Even Australian hippies appeared inauthentic to me, like some kind of rip-off for public voyeurism. Australia's efforts to imitate American products or customs usually came off poorly. America's future will undeniably affect the policies of other nations: its problems will in all probability, reappear elsewhere; its successes are likely to be merchandized abroad before the first television commercial announcing their arrival has been completed.

Australian values can often be as empty or as uplifting as the American variety. Both nations value materialism and both admire their frontier heroes, except that ours is named Billy the Kid and theirs, Ned Kelly. They also share a Horatio Alger tradition and a spirit of "fair play." Yet it is the United Stated that remains the unpredictable factor, the state whose destiny continents like Australia depend on.

As I recall my Australian experience, I also remember the story included in Race and Nationality in American Life about the Italian immigrant who continually told his American friends how wonderful it was in the old country. After years of saving, he finally had enough money to return to Italy. But it wasn't the Italy he had expected. In fact, it didn't compare with the America he has been criticizing all these years. The author of the book, Oscar Handlin, concluded that this story, which has been retold in many second-generation homes, is like the one about the young man who gets married and, for the first time in his life, comes to appreciate his mother.

Australia had a similar effect on me. That period abroad gave me a new perspective. I realize that there is something magical about the United States. I may still take many things for granted, and at times I do feel the urge to demolish the government and start over again, but that feeling is certainly less frequent since my voyage to Australia. It helps, I believe, to understand America from the land down under.

Chapter Two

How a Commencement Changed My Life

It was a sunny day in May 1971 with flowers in bloom as the NYU commencement ceremony was about to begin in Washington Square Park. God seemed to smile on this event since it hadn't rained on commencement day in the decade since the university decided to hold this ceremony outdoors.

Parents and grandparents waited patiently on line as bagpipers marched down University Place setting the stage for the ceremony that was about to begin.

There weren't any surprises for me. The event followed the libretto. Several students jumped into the fountain consistent with the temper of the times. But there weren't any political demonstrations of the kind I had grown familiar with on previous occasions.

What did strike me as notable was President James Hester's address. Clearly university presidents are inclined to exaggerate. After all, why be in the business of education unless you believe and can assert that it makes a difference. But on this occasion I felt the president went too far, beyond the point of realistic reference.

He said, "We have seated before us a class of students prepared to solve the issues of war and peace, income disparity and urban woe." Now, I taught some of these students who often objected to reading a 250 page book. I recalled that in the three preceding years the Spring semester became an interlude from academic work so that demonstrations and bacchanalian pleasures could be entertained. I remembered that many students spent more time scoring drugs in Washington Square Park than reading in the library.

How does one square the platitudes pronounced at this occasion with the reality of this student population? I was flummoxed. Leaving the park I inadvertently ran into President Hester, who asked me what I thought of his remarks. Unable to resist an honest response, I noted that it was silly to make claims of the kind he did when you cannot be certain these students ever read a serious book.

Looking askance at me, the president asked, "What would you say?" "Well, I'd tone down the phony expectations and at the very least would make sure that students read great books."

That exchange fraught with manifest frustration, was the beginning of a great change in my professional life. Until that moment I had mixed feelings about my university appointment. I found university politics boring. As Henry Kissinger once noted, so much passion goes into trivial things, in part because there is so little at stake. I found the students, with rare exception, to be uninterested, despite my ardent attempt to generate enthusiasm for historical study. And I discovered my colleagues often spent more time worrying about sabbaticals than concentrating on their discipline.

Therefore it was not coincidental that I sought employment outside the Academy. Since the *Saturday Review* of that era was breaking up into four magazines, one on education, I applied to be editor of that publication.

It was also about the time that President Hester organized a committee to examine undergraduate education and I was appointed to this group. Did my commencement conversation with James Hester have anything to do with the appointment? I can only speculate.

After several meetings led by then Vice President L. Jay Oliva, we were advised to break up into subcommittees, a reflexive academic response, I believe. I was assigned to a subcommittee originally entitled "The College Alternative." Where I grew up, the college alternative was work. But this after all, was the so-called arrival of a "new age."

Over vino and baked clams at The Grand Ticino, a restaurant otherwise known as NYU West, Michael Miller, the associate dean in the Tisch School of the Arts, and I brainstormed—when the vino allowed our brains to storm—about a new college at the university. I wrote a proposal, which Mike revised. We shared this idea with the whole committee and, with minor changes, it found its way into the final report.[1] At this point, I thought my job was completed. Little did I know that this was arguably the only committee in university history whose report had consequences—for me, for many students and for the university.

Several weeks after the undergraduate committee disbanded, I read in a university newspaper that a decision had been made for NYU to join a consortium of experimenting colleges. The director of the NYU program, known as the University Without Walls, was L. Jay Oliva. Each college in the consortium received a grant of $25,000—money provided by the Department of Education and the Ford Foundation. Several days after I read this article, the director of the fledging UWW called to ask if I would be interested in being its director. At first I was baffled. After all, this was a university without walls, without faculty and without students. It's a little difficult to administer a program without these fundamental resources. But I did have $25,000, the support of the vice president and a plan created under the influence of Italian wine.

My first request as director was for walls. This was easier said than done. Since space was at a premium in the university—some things never change—Vice President Oliva suggested that we use two dormitory spaces for the UWW office. What I didn't know at the time was that these offices were in Rubin Hall, a dormitory for women. While there were undoubtedly desirable features to this arrangement, I was required to have an escort to our third-floor offices, and I was obliged to notify my floor neighbors of my presence should they decide to prance around the corridors without the accompaniment of bathroom attire. Needless to say, every office visit was an adventure.

In the first year, seventeen intrepid students decided to enroll in the division. These people will forever have my gratitude. What they expressed was a confidence in a nontraditional program that afforded a flexible arrangement for study with traditional standards of academic rigor. As a dedicated traditionalist, I was probably the wrong candidate for the job of director. I wasn't comfortable with the zeitgeist in the seventies, and it soon became apparent that the avatars in the experimental consortium had a view of the nontraditional very different from mine. When I wrote an article for *Saturday Review* decrying most educational experiments as ideas without substance, I was drummed out of the nontraditional fraternity. Experimentation, it turns our, has an ironically rigid orthodoxy of its own.

It was, and is, my belief that the "delivery system" of education may vary without harm to the enterprise, but there are well understood goals with which one tampers at great peril to the educational process. Whether students sign contracts, learn through video programs or experience, engage in seminars or simply spend time in the library is, in the final analysis, less significant than what they know and what they can do. In this sense, my approach to learning is pragmatic. I simply want to be sure that students who gained degrees from this division demonstrate the research capacity and knowledge one would associate with the graduates from the nation's most prestigious colleges. In fact, as I told President Hester, I wanted to make sure that at the very least students read "great books."

As I organized the program, with marvelous colleagues, who were, as Dean Acheson might put it, "present at the creation," a general education requirement of sixty points was replaced by great books and classic texts requirements. Students in the division to this day don't have to take philosophy, for example, but they must read Plato and Aristotle and demonstrate at an oral exam that they are familiar with the works of these authors. The great books requirement is one dimension of the activities that set us apart from all other nontraditional programs. In fact, it also set us apart from many traditional programs.

Although I was satisfied with what we were trying to accomplish, most faculty members at NYU had a justifiably jaundiced view of educational experiments. If there was one moment when attitudes toward the UWW changed slightly, it was at a Faculty Council meeting in 1972. As I was explaining my goals, Professor Sidney Hook, distinguished professor of philosophy, interrupted my remarks and inquired if a great person ever graduated from an external degree program. So nonplussed was I by this question that I couldn't think of a great person who graduated from a *traditional* college program. Moreover, Professor Hook had apparently confused my description with an external degree program, which the UWW decidedly was not. However, Professor Hook was waiting for an answer. Reaching into my memory bank, where trivia about everything from the etymology of "brouhaha" to George Kell's career batting average aimlessly swim about, I blurted out, "Lenin." Now Lenin is not a great man in my opinion, an opinion with which Professor Hook concurred. However, he looked at me in astonishment and asked, "How do you know that?" I said, "Lenin attended the University of Moscow extension division. I remember reading that fact in Bertram Wolfe's *Three Who Made a Revolution*." At that point Professor Hook noted, "Anyone who knows that deserves my support." In 1973 and 1974, before his retirement from this university, Professor Hook advised UWW students. In 1973, we collaborated on a book entitled *The Philosophy of Education*. As an inveterate opponent of revolution, Professor Hook helped to create one at NYU.

There were still battles to fight and few allies available. Unfortunately, Professor Hook left NYU to write his books from an office at the Hoover Institute, but his involvement in this program proved to be very significant for its future. While there were faculty members and students in other colleges who asked quizzically what our enterprise did, we had by any standard made an indelible mark on the history of NYU.

In 1976, this program metamorphosed into a division with two hundred students. We introduced a Master's program, a weekend college, a great artist program, a public policy lecture series and a writing program, which at last count has produced sixteen published novels. By 1987 our enrollment rose to almost seven hundred students. The UWW program was renamed to honor Albert Gallatin and to reflect his iconoclastic nature. It was Gallatin who, as one of the founders of NYU, argued that New York City needed a college for the children of merchants instead of another elite institution to train ministers, as was the case at Kings College (later Columbia). When asked if New York

College students would study Greek and Latin like their Kings College counterparts, he said, "No." When asked if these students would study English, Gallatin the inveterate nationalist, smiled and said, "In my college students will study American." He was my kind of politician.

For twenty-odd years I served as dean. There is no doubt Gallatin had found a place on the NYU map during that period. But it is still evolving. Some may recall that Gertrude Stein posed more than two years for Picasso. Finally, rather exasperated at not seeing her portrait, she implored the master for a look. Picasso reluctantly agreed. When Stein saw her portrait, she reportedly said with great annoyance, "That doesn't look like me!" Picasso, without skipping a beat, said, "Gertrude, it will, it will!" Well, I couldn't have drawn a portrait of Gallatin twenty years ago, nor can I draw one today. However, that portrait is not what I thought it might be and its resemblance to my original conception of Gallatin is merely coincidental. More about that in the succeeding pages.

NOTE

1. Report of the Commission on Undergraduate Education.

Chapter Three

Running to Class

As I've already noted, most of my first two years at Columbia were a blur. I worked in the early morning, went to class until 4 PM and then practiced on the basketball court till 7. Frankly, I didn't know if I was coming or going. Confusion reigned.

By the time I reached the cafeteria, where I stood behind the counter and served, my eyelids were in full retreat. Pancakes were served as waffles and eggs benedict became scrambled.

But some thoughts about professors remained etched in my imagination. Daniel Bell was a disorganized, but brilliant, lecturer. It was obvious that he was a visionary whose work on the *Post Industrial Society* and *The Cultural Contradictions of Capitalism* extended and elaborated on the ideas of Joseph Schumpeter.

Carl Van Doren was a gifted teacher, whose expository writing class was among my favorites. However, when he fell from grace over a fraudulent quiz show, I was deeply disappointed.

Samuel Huntington was an odd selection as an adviser. As I recall, he said, "You can take any set of courses. If you are serious, you might learn something." It wasn't exactly an unvarnished vote of confidence. In fact, I sensed that this kind of advisement wasn't his cup of tea. In later years, he advised indirectly through his many books, including *The Conflict of Civilizations and Who Are We*?

Amitai Etzioni impressed me as a passionate theoretician honing his thoughts into a world view that ultimately became the "new communitarianism."

William Casey, the doyen of social thought, introduced me to concepts such as mechanical mimesis and the underpinnings of ancient Greek culture. Many years later, I met H. D. F. Kitto, the author of *The Greeks*, who told me how much he admired William Casey. I shared that admiration. Professor

Casey even took a personal interest in me, a condition that rarely occurred at Columbia. He often attended basketball games and commented on my performance. Thank God those conversations didn't take place in class.

The person who had the greatest influence on me was Jacques Barzun. Watching him in a classroom was like watching Fred Astaire on film. He was elegant, in control, self-effacing, brilliant. I rarely spoke in his class, but I observed and recorded every move he made in the hope I might emulate him one day. His was the one class I would always run to. I wasn't willing to miss a word he uttered.

Years later Professor Barzun asked me to join him for lunch at the Century Club. He had a proposition: A book he wrote, *The American University*, was being reissued by the University of Chicago Press. Since the book was published in 1967, Professor Barzun asked if I would write a "brief" introduction bringing the history up-to-date. More flattered than he could possibly realize, I agreed. Moreover, I assumed the introduction would only be a few pages.

About this assumption, I would soon be disabused. Barzun said, somewhat sheepishly, "I'd like you to write a history based on your experience in the Academy. Oh, something like a hundred pages. Yes, of course, I will pay you for it in the form of royalties." I gulped. One, I wasn't prepared for an assignment of this magnitude and, two, I was so flattered by the offer that compensation could not compare to the psychic reward. I agreed to write this opus over the summer months.

Jacques took this commitment literally. On September 1, I received a call inquiring about the manuscript. I gulped again, this time noting that the summer didn't end till September 21. For the following three weeks I worked furiously on this document not wanting to disappoint my hero. When it was finished, my former professor said, "now our work begins." In painstaking fashion he went over every word demanding justification for certain constructions and syntactical usage. I felt very much like a student again, and when our work was completed and the book published, I took great pride in the fact that Jacques Barzun approved of my scholarship.

This was not our only interesting encounter. As a dean in the university, I was obliged to raise funds for the college. It was as a fundraiser that I approached a Mr. Charles Carlyle, public affairs director at St. Joe's Minerals. We met at his Park Avenue office, and I mentally prepared to make my pitch as I waited in the foyer of his office. However, when we met, he disarmingly said, "I don't like academics. They are so damn pompous." At this point, I thought it best to turn around and leave. Instead I blurted out, "I agree with you." "No you don't," he insisted. "I'll bet you don't know what expression academics use that demonstrates their pomposity." Without hesitation, I noted that I do know. "The phrase you are referring to is "in terms of," a phrase that rarely refers to terms." Mr. Carlyle had the strangest look on his face. "In all the years I've been behind this desk, I've never met anyone who knew that. At this point I told Carlyle that as a student of Jacques Barzun, I read about the test of pomposity in his book, *Teacher in America*. Although a difficult man to impress, Carlyle seemed quite satisfied with that explanation. In fact, he took out a corporate check and made it out to my N.Y.U. school for $35,000. He said, "this is for you, but don't come back again."

    The first thing I did upon leaving that office was call Jacques Barzun. "Jacques," I said, "not only have I learned a great deal from you, but now I can say I've profited from that learning." The full story was recounted as I walked down Park Avenue with a smile on my face. I also promised myself I would never use the expression "in terms of.

Chapter Four

Underground Notes from a Campus Ombudsman

Looking back over my university experience, there is probably no role that better prepared me to serve as dean more than my tenure as university ombudsman. It was in this position that I learned about the fragility of faculty egos, the compensatory assertiveness of students and the byzantine administration of the university.

After holding the post for only two weeks, I decided that the title "ombudsman" did not reflect my new role. I was no longer a mere mortal, I was an om-*batman,* with the emphasis on the last two syllables. In only two weeks time, I realized that the alleged defender of student rights was also a supersleuth, a consultant, a psychologist and a mediator. I also asked myself repeatedly whether students really needed a defender and if I should be in that position.

With the announcement of my election, every student with a legitimate grievance (is there a student without a legitimate grievance?) could now relieve his burden by discussing it with the ombudsman. From where I was sitting there did not appear to be too many shirkers. In hordes they came for relief, absolution, help and to satisfy their curiosity. Flattered at first, I rose to the challenge by indiscriminately listening to every complainant. After a week of ritualistic acknowledgments, I found my own research suffering, my neck stiff and my wife looking at me in disbelief as I related tales of indiscretion and woe. When I told the dean of my plight, he said to "establish guidelines" for the job—bureaucratese for being selective. In an effort to be selective, I referred students to appropriate university offices. As I expected, some of them returned to my desk with a look on their faces that was at once quizzical and angry. In most cases they just stared at me and then blurted out, "Cop-out. How could you just pass the buck? Don't you know nothing ever gets done in that other office?" My response was a sheepish, "I just can't do everything," as I weakly raised a hand that denoted a halfhearted *c'est la vie.*

At those moments, I asked myself what had I gotten into. I'm not sure there is an appropriate answer to the question. However, after my abortive attempt to establish procedures, I was sure that whatever an ombudsman was, he certainly was not a buck passer. Once again my door was open and once again the hordes appeared; an experience, I thought, that just served to legitimate Parkinson's law. Perhaps it is necessary at this point to explain how I got involved in this dilemma in the first place.

Having been convinced by Hannah Arendt that large bureaucratic institutions like the one that employs me are often insensitive to student grievances, a point I have come to reexamine, I was already predisposed to the idea of a campus ombudsman before the matter ever came up. From personal experience I felt reasonably sure that thoughtless bureaucratic decisions were usually not the fault of administrators, who on the whole are about as thoughtful as the faculties from which they come, but of a spiraling bureaucratization that dispersed responsibility and decision making until it was impossible to determine how decisions were made and who was responsible for enforcing them. An ombudsman could cut the red tape, or at least I thought so, if he were given a free hand to represent aggrieved students, thereby locating and remedying flaws in the bureaucratic system.

At the end of the previous academic year, several student leaders approached me about the possibility of my being a nominee for the position (students were permitted one nomination and the faculty three). Since I had been engaged in postdoctoral study out of the country for some time and had cautiously guarded my anonymity upon returning to the university, I thought my nomination was due more to my age (under thirty at the time) than to any special qualification for the role. I accepted the nomination, thinking that my anonymity militated against my election. And I was correct.

Losing the election was a disappointment, since I secretly coveted the role more than I admitted. But on the other hand I could rationalize the loss by daydreaming about an ombudsman drowning in a sea of paper work. Both these hopes and fears were reawakened when the victor resigned from the position one month after his election and a special runoff among the remaining candidates was conducted. This time, no rationalization or disappointment was forthcoming. I was elected, by the narrowest of margins; I was now the ombudsman.

No trumpets blared as I entered my office the following day. In fact, there was no change in my life at all for several days, aside from a few congratulatory and some snide commiserative messages. Not one student had come to complain. When the vice dean called to negotiate (his word) my released time for "my new responsibilities," I could not argue very forcefully for more than six load units for the job (a little more than one-third of my university commitment and less than the recommendation made by the representative student organizations), since for all practical purposes I did not have a new job.

This would all change more quickly than I care to remember. Seven months later I was still recovering from the "ombudsman bends," an occupational hazard I'd discovered. My exposure to my constituents began when the editor of the *Graduate Students' Organization Newsletter* wrote an article about my personal background and the responsibilities of the job. From some very undisciplined reading about the Scandinavian and New Zealand ombudsmen, I had a vague idea of the role, but the article was my first exposure to the expectations for a campus ombudsman. In bold print I read, the ombudsman "shall be authorized to examine any complaint brought to him by a student or a group of students of his college" and "shall be authorized to call for a review of any decision of any official or committee, or of any decision of any official or committee, or of the faculty, that is related to the complaint, and to appeal to higher authority when the possibility exists, but he shall not be authorized to alter said decision by his own action alone." How this directive would be related to my actual functions I just couldn't know, but with the publication of the article and the subsequent arrival of complainants I had my first chance to find out.

Being compulsively conscientious about my new position, I was determined to find out what other ombudsmen had done—before deciding what I should do, through the lessons imbibed in my own trial and error. The literature revealed the role as a mixed bag. Some ombudsmen were often another arm of the administration and were branded by student militants as "a tool of the establishment." Others were initiators of student activism, using the role as a soapbox for SDS-style rhetoric. Still others, with a keenly developed sense of morality, viewed the position as the university's conscience and proceeded to act like cloistered Benedictines.

The mode of operation was also different at different schools. Some ombudsmen kept their doors open twelve hours a day in an effort to deal with the traffic of student complaints, while others had only a handful of cases each year requiring no more than ten hours a semester of the ombudsman's time.

The literature shows that opinions about the value of ombudsman mediation also vary. Earle W. Clifford, dean of students at Rutgers, compared the ombudsman "to putting a penny in the fuse socket when a circuit blows." He has argued, "A decision to go the ombudsman route is a fine advertisement for the failure of an administration in general or a student personnel program in particular to meet responsibilities for equity and communication in an academic community." Yet even when it is admitted that an ombudsman is little more than a palliative in situations that require dramatic reform, most observers would agree the position can mitigate certain disagreeable conditions and, at times, even potentially explosive conflicts on the campus. A city ombudsman has noted that an ombudsman can isolate aberrations in the bureaucratic system, suggest ways of reaching mutually agreed upon ends and point out new applications of institutional functions.

It is also apparent that the ombudsman is perceived differently by different groups and individuals on the campus. Since he is presumably an independent, and in some ways privileged, force on the campus, he has the power to interfere with the prerogatives of students, faculty, and administrators. If he deals with student grievances expeditiously and fairly, he can prevent minor student irritations from growing into major grievances. In a survey by Howard Ray Rowland at Michigan State University, two-thirds of those students who consulted the university's ombudsman felt he helped relieve frustration and hostility. However, since the ombudsman tries to make the university's bureaucratic system function efficiently, he aids in the retention of the status quo, a situation that has led to his condemnation by some nihilistic students.

The faculty at many universities is equally ambivalent about the position. Undoubtedly the ombudsman in the pursuit of justice for aggrieved students will often challenge faculty decisions. No matter how discreet his handling of a case may be, there are times when circumstances will force him into the position of impinging on academic freedom. (This was borne out by my own experience several times.) In these cases, a residual resentment often proscribes future ombudsman-faculty relations, since the rumor mill, a potent force at most American colleges, will portray him as a threat to the "inviolable principle" of academic freedom and a person to be tolerated, but not encouraged. Fortunately, most faculties cooperate with their ombudsman, but his potential for restricting their rights very often inhibits their enthusiastic acceptance of the position. Interestingly, ombudsmen get almost unanimous endorsement from administrators. This is obviously not due to the enlightened view of the university that is engendered by accepting an administrative office. It was probably a concomitant of the administration's hang-up about keeping the campus calm during turbulent student days of the 1970s. As has already been noted, it is rather doubtful that an ombudsman can prevent student disruptions initiated and controlled by messianic radicals. But he can often restrain the liberal majority from joining the radicals by reducing the student alienation that is usually a factor in the political coalitions that can paralyze a university. In the adjudication of legitimate grievances he can create the impression someone does care; at many campuses that is all the students really want anyway. In addition, an ombudsman patently reduces the work load, the "burdensome chore" of dealing with students, formerly reserved for administrators, particularly the dean of students. It is quite likely an ombudsman will refer students to administrative offices, but those that leave him have already been screened, and their complaints have been deemed sufficiently serious to warrant further investigation. At some universities the "student protector" is no more than an administrative ploy to reduce the proliferating headaches encountered each day.

On one point there does seem to be consensus about the role: students, professors, and administrators have agreed that the ombudsman should have "knowledge of campus operations and regulations, understanding, effectiveness, authority and accessibility." At the University of California at Berkeley, one member of the academic senate summarized the criteria by suggesting the ombudsman have "a pair of wings and a halo."

After my examination of the literature, I was more convinced than ever that I was conspicuously unqualified for the role: I am not diplomatic in my relations with colleagues, an indispensable criterion for an ombudsman; my institutional commitment is directly related to the courses I am permitted to teach, to administrative cooperation with my research projects, to financial assistance, to released time and to salary increments; my concern for students is related to their willingness to use rational and thoughtful processes for the solution of problems, quite an anachronistic notion at this time; and I am not particularly tolerant of students who have no real grievances, only those they have been able to fabricate. In referring to the specific role criteria cited by all groups on the campus, I could argue an unfamiliarity with the operation and regulations of the school, a philosophical gap with the more activist students, a lack of authority that was partially a function of being unknown among most of my colleagues, and an ineffectiveness in handling administrative matters, which I attributed rather blindly to inexperience at that time.

Recognizing, somewhat clearly I think, my unpreparedness for the post, I was still eager to handle my first ombudsman case. As it turned out, it was more eventful than I anticipated. An elderly woman in her sixties led a moderately attractive young lady into my office and introduced herself as the complainant's mother. She then proceeded to explain the details of the alleged grievance as her daughter sat silently and stared at my maps of the world. For one hour, I heard this mother rant about the unfairness in the school and about the young professors jealous of her daughter's ability. But I was unable to discern a problem until the daughter interrupted her mother for the first time and said, "What my mother has neglected to say is that the chairman won't accept me into the guidance program." The words "guidance program" were mind boggling. This young girl who was still obviously entangled in her mother's apron strings wanted to counsel others. Trying to avoid prejudicial statements, which were hard to restrain, I addressed my questions to the girl, who was much less objectionable than her garrulous mother. However, every question was answered by Mom. "What qualifications do you have to pursue a graduate degree in that department?" I asked. "Why, professor, don't you know my daughter is a member of Mensa." All I could say was, "Congratulations. I think you deserve each other." As they were leaving under the continuous pressure of my right arm, I promised to investigate the matter further.

The very next day, I called an adviser in the guidance program for an appointment. After mentioning my name several times to no avail, I yielded to impulse and said, "The ombudsman is calling." My appointment was scheduled for that afternoon. As I suspected, most of the department's professors thought the young lady's academic performance was satisfactory, but doubted she had the maturity to be an adequate baby-sitter. In an effort to be fair, one professor remarked, "Let her reapply when she shows signs of growing up."

Despite my displeasure, I called the young lady to tell her she might reapply in "a semester or two"—I wasn't sure how long it takes to "grow up." But her mother answered the phone, and before I could deliver my message, notified me that her daughter had left for Europe "to work things out and find herself." Case closed, at least temporarily.

Just as I hung up the phone, my secretary informed me, "A very angry woman is here to see the ombudsman." For reasons I can't explain, everyone I knew referred to me in the third person and I replied the same way. "Tell her the ombudsman will see her in five minutes."

Once again, a middle-aged woman came into the office. I was beginning to think I had a strange attraction for mothers. Before I could introduce myself, she raged, "I've never suffered such indignities in my life. I must have satisfaction." "What happened?" I asked meekly, fearful that her flailing arms might hit me in the stomach. "You'll never believe this. I've been attending this university for ten years and never have I been treated so discourteously. A professor at least ten years my junior had the nerve to refer to me as Sadie instead of Mrs. Perlman." (The names have been changed for obvious reasons.) I feigned seriousness about the charge, promised immediate satisfaction, closed my door, and shook my head in despair.

When I told one member of the administration about these cases, he said, "The crazy ones now have a new office to bring their complaints to." It was obvious the kooks were coming, and I wasn't sure whether I was coming or going. In my feeble effort to describe my duties to a colleague, I wrote the following note, which was later attached to my office door: "He hears about your woe, investigates your problem, and finds a magic remedy. He is your counsel, friend, confidante. Please don't be disturbed by the thunder you hear in his presence."

One of my students attached this inscription to the sign: "Is he a shrink, the fuzz, or Underdog? No! He's Ombatman!" After my experience with the next grievant, I was fairly sure some students mistakenly regarded me as "a shrink."

A plain girl with very thick glasses and stains all over her blouse requested some advice from the ombudsman. She wanted to know whether it was appropriate to give a professor a gift. This hardly seemed a matter that I should be concerned with, but her urgency made me attentive. "Why are you seeking advice from me" I asked. "Surely it would be advisable to discuss this with your professor." For an extended minute she just stared into space; finally she said, "I really wanted to get your impression of the gift." She slipped a white card out of a carrying case and showed it to me. The card was constructed like a triptych, with each section having what seemed to be a globe and a fetus. "What is the significance of the drawing?" I inquired innocently. "Significance? Significance?" she replied, each word becoming more faint. Again she stared out into space blankly, in what I considered a catatonic trance. No other words were uttered; after several minutes she just left without a farewell. As soon as she departed, I called a university psychiatrist and described the incident. He must have contacted her, had several interviews and placed her in his care, for two months later I learned from the clinic that the young lady was under "intensive care" and had made "a dramatic improvement."

I was soon to learn that most student grievances were of a very different variety. Some involved the length of time it takes to process a transcript of grades; others were concerned with refunds the university neglected to pay; still others dealt with the lack of sufficient security police to cope with the violence directed at evening students. For several weeks, I was clerk, secretary, bursar and security policeman. I spent as much time in the recording office as in my classes. And, to my surprise, the expenditure of time paid off: I soon realized that the real "bureaucratic problem" at the university is the surly clerk who is unconcerned about any student requests, even the most legitimate ones. This unseen and relatively unheard of woman (most of the time, a single girl who is attentive only to the more handsome male graduate students) is the real scourge of the university. She possesses virtually unlimited power over students and, more importantly, is usually not supervised by administrators. For all practical purposes she has as much control over students' graduation as any faculty member and, from my own observation, is accorded more respect by students.

The kind of case I relished dealt with the quality of teaching and course offerings. If there is one thing an ombudsman should be concerned with, it is the presumptive university goal: educating its students. When this did not happen satisfactorily, I was prepared to jump into the nearest telephone booth (yes, there were telephone booths in 1968), change into my work clothes, and fly into action.

One consequence of the job was discovering which colleagues prepare for class sessions, attend class, are inebriated in class, are indiscreet with students and are trying to seduce every sweet thing in a miniskirt. It was just the kind of data needed for a new Edward Albee play, but with the exception of my wife, I didn't break the faith.

Several fellowship students arrived in my office to complain about A's. This was certainly a new one on me. In a "special program" (you can always tell a special program by the especially large number of complaints) designed for these students, they were asked to take a semester of independent study in which specially tailored projects were pursued. However, students claimed they had no supervision, requirements, papers, conferences, seminars, or anything else. They were just "given a vacation"—as they put it—and rewarded with A's.

Another student, complaining about a grade, described a formula his professor used for grade determination (the very fact "a formula" existed made me sympathetic to the student). However, at the end of the semester his grade was lower than his accumulated average. I called the professor and was told that in the middle of the semester he decided to change the formula, without informing the class of the revision. When I diplomatically suggested that this oversight might have penalized some students, he said, "Who the hell are you to interfere with my academic freedom?" Case closed. It was obvious that a few professors used academic freedom as an excuse for almost any ill-advised action.

Still another student told of a class in which the professor allegedly, without informing the class or providing for a substitute, missed the first four sessions. The student demanded a refund, a request that was quite unprecedented, but seemingly justified. In order to avoid the embarrassing effects of a hearing with a tenured faculty member, the administration had the refund made.

The issue of race has generated considerable anxiety at almost every university worthy of its name. At my school, things had been fairly quiet, which is testimony to either an unworthy university, fairness, a docile student body, the lack of controversy or a sensitive faculty. I've attributed the condition to the faculty. As a faculty member who can easily be placed in the middle of a confrontation, I've been particularly sensitive to the issue. Perhaps that explained why I was solicitous about the first charge of racism directed at a faculty member. Mr. Gomez (the name has been changed), a Puerto Rican student, reported "racist conditions in a Spanish class that were "so humiliating" he could not "perform as expected." He provided little evidence to substantiate this serious charge except a disagreement over dialect, which hardly constituted signs of racism, and a grade of D, which the student argued was unwarranted. The episode that followed clearly points up the problem often faced by a faculty member who is "color blind."

According to the records, Mr. Gomez received a numerical grade of 33 on the final exam, which, the professor noted, accounts for two-thirds of the grade. Since Mr. Gomez compiled a *C* average on other papers and quizzes, the final grade seemed fair, albeit the average gives you no idea at all of the grading on any one test. I, therefore, felt obliged to let a friend examine the final exam paper; he thought the grade was generous. What I did not know at the time was why Gomez challenged the grade. But at a later meeting, he noted that his perspective of the incident was affected by his grade in a graduate linguistics course. Here he achieved an 11 on the final, did poorly in his class work and by every indicator deserved to fail, yet he received a *C* as a final grade. When questioned about this, the professor said quite candidly, "I want to avoid charges of racial discrimination and maintain good ties with the Puerto Rican community. Sure he deserved to fail, but no harm will come of the *C*."

When I told Mr. Gomez his charges were unfounded, he screamed, "I will get satisfaction somewhere. This is an insult to my name, my family, my people, and my nation." I did not hear from him again.

The most unforgettable student I met during my term in office was poor Mr. Chang (the name has been changed, and I assure you the "poor" is not a sign of condescension). This student has been in and out of every administrative office at the university; he would speak to any receptive listener, and he would go on interminably about his tale of woe. He was one of the most charming and articulate students I've ever met, and if the paintings he showed me were any indication, he may also have been among the most talented.

Mr. Chang came to see me about the grade of Incomplete obtained in an art history class. According to his description, he was asked to do a "special project" in his area of expertise –Chinese silk-screen painting—which was tantamount to writing a popular book. Since he was unable to complete the project at the end of the semester, he did not challenge the grade. What complicated matters, though, was that his inability to complete the project the following semester would mean the Incomplete would automatically become an *F*. As a result, he would lose his state scholarship, he would jeopardize his standing in the department, his degree would be prolonged, and he would be unable to obtain financial assistance for his ailing mother in Hong Kong. Now you see why he was "poor" Mr. Chang; every day was hazardous for him. One day his typewriter broke down, preventing him from further work on his project; another day, the plethora of notes, which he carried everywhere, was blowing in a New York wind.

To be insensitive to his plight was impossible, I thought. I soon found out differently. Clerks "detested him" because he invariably registered late for courses, a sin long remembered by women forced to leave their offices five minutes later than usual. That this was a function of his poverty was conspicuously forgotten by those encountered. In fact, Mr. Chang was selling canvasses up to the last moment of registration. Several administrators said he was "a nuisance, always hanging around the place." Sure he was; but no one paid any attention to him anyway. A faculty member remarked, "Oh, Chang. He can bring tears to anyone's eyes; that's how he gets away with murder." I was unable to determine what murder he was getting away with.

Chang's professor denied asking him to write a book. "All I wanted," he claimed, "was an outline." Chang presented written evidence in the professor's hand indicating otherwise. In addition, Chang argued he had already completed several chapters of the book, which he felt could be substituted for term papers. However, "a congenital oriental self-effacement" (his description) prevented him from meeting with the professor or letting him read the chapters; and pride, as well as "academic freedom," were reasons the professor gave for being firm. As I saw it, the only way to cut the Gordian knot was to negotiate a compromise that might offend the professor without alienating him completely. I asked the chairman whether Chang could use his completed chapters to eliminate the Incomplete and finish his project as "independent study," while maintaining his matriculation in the department. He agreed, even though the professor bitterly reproved the action.

Mr. Chang still registered late, I was told, and is still castigated by clerks, but he didn't care so much anymore. He contended that he had a special friend who looked out for him. I treasured that friendship.

Not all of the cases have such happy endings. Several weeks after the Chang affair, a girl, with a voice reminiscent of Marilyn Monroe, requested a "very private talk" with the ombudsman. Her complaint (I don't think that accurately describes it) was that one of her professors was trying to seduce her. A basic shyness, I guess, inhibited me from asking perceptive questions. I said, "What evidence do you have?" "Well," she hesitated for a moment, "he has asked me out to lunch. And even though we weren't alone, he did stare at me. And those eyes; he has this way of looking at me . . . ." Stupidly, I asked her to describe the look as she proceeded to contort every muscle in her face. It was perfectly obvious, to me at any rate, that this girl was projecting and imposing her fantasies on her most recent captive audience. I don't doubt seductions do occur with ever-increasing frequency at the school, but I felt positive that no one was seducing this young lady. Losing my cool for a minute, I scolded, "If you have no better evidence than a look, I suggest you find some." She did not waste any time leaving my office. I've discovered that tact is not always my strong suit.

One decision that did have significant ramifications for the school was the announcement of new rules governing the English competency exam. The exam is a requirement for master's degree candidates, an indication of basic literacy. You may be asking why this kind of exam is a requisite for an MA. I was asking the same question, too; but I didn't have any satisfactory answer. What I do know is that while the exam is required during the first semester, the ruling is not enforced. Consequently, there were students who have satisfactorily completed their degree requirements, but could not graduate. And passing the exam is not so easy for our students. In the five years before my tenure in the university, more than 50 percent failed the exam the first time they took it. For many students, it seemed as though an artificial hurdle had been manufactured that they must jump. It is particularly irritating to those who had been writing satisfactory term papers in their courses to be told "a writing test is necessary to prove your English competency."

Much of the blame for this irritation can be directed at advisers. If they were to administer the program as mandated, there would have been no problem. However, another fact of university life is that many program advisers are power builders. They view their success by the number of people enrolled in *their* program. Significantly, many of these people do not attend faculty meetings where decisions about the exam are made, and they are accustomed, without an extended glance, to deposit all memorandums in the same filing cabinet day after day. A time was fast approaching when few would know the school regulations and even fewer would care. Faculty meetings will be designed for their cathartic effect, and business will be delegated to those unseen and uncaring clerks who keep accumulating more power.

Fortunately, students complained, a dean acted, and I negotiated. It was anticipated that the following year there would be some sanity introduced into the exam procedures. However, I think it's fruitless to do anything about most program advisers, except relieve them of their responsibilities, and that is precisely what I recommended—even though I knew I'd be charged with overstepping the bounds of my authority.

Despite some obvious cynicism, I came to believe a campus ombudsman might be necessary. Just what the role involves is still hard to say. A friend of mine described me as a "high-grade hydrant." Well, at least I can take comfort in being high grade, a point I could not make as a dean years later.

Most universities are now suffering through a period of ombudsmania. Every time there is a campus crisis, some group asks for an ombudsman. Well, it is doubtful that he can solve all the problems, as my own experience indicated; it is even doubtful the most serious problems will be negotiated through his office. One obvious conclusion from my term (and I doubt whether you can generalize from it) is that militant students seeking political ends on the campus do not see the ombudsman. Those who came generally had personal problems whose solution did not jeopardize the future of the university. The extent of private grief that never came to the ombudsman's attention, or for that matter anyone's attention, is probably astounding. If he does no more than listen, the ombudsman performs an invaluable service for the university, or at least, I think this might be the case.

Chapter Five

What a Dean Learns from His Mother

Lest one get the wrong impression, I became a dean because I founded a college. My suspicion is I wasn't good material for my decanal status. I am strong-willed, have deeply held convictions and do not suffer fools easily. In most instances, deans are hydrants, urinated on by those below and above.

Yet there I was, a dean who had little patience for academic politics and who adhered to the belief that deans should defend the traditions on which the Academy depended. But I was in the eye of a hurricane. Woodstock Nation visited NYU with a vengeance.

The Spring semester, as I pointed out, could accurately be described as a bacchanalian respite since classes were suspended from 1968 to 1972.

Student radicals, I met very few who weren't at least sympathetic to the radicals, dominated campus life at this time and they were intent on bringing their anti–Vietnam War position to the campus.

What surprised me and, in fact still evokes astonishment, is the extent to which faculty members succumbed to student pressure. That my colleagues could be so pusillanimous in the face of student intimidation was startling. Courses were student led, faculty members often looked to students for guidance as if these kids were the Red Guard, and even the university senate recognized students as a constituency equal to the faculty. One might well have asked: If these students know so much, why are they in the university to learn. And if faculty and students are equal in what some described as the "new democratic setting," how can judgments about student performance be made?

Alas, these judgments were made as undifferentiated grading for students was put in place and as students were put in the position of evaluating their professors. As I see it, this was comparable to a new version of Thomas

Mann's *Magic Mountain* in which the patients ran the institution for the insane.

On one occasion, I was chastised by a student group for being an "elitist." Presumable an elitist was someone who had undeviating standards and a sense of academic tradition. One day, there was a sign in front of the building in which my office was located that said "London is elitist." When I saw this sign, my initial reaction is that the British had a sense of *noblesse oblige*. It didn't occur to me that I was being criticized for the maintenance of standards.

On yet another occasion, I was told by a group of self appointed Red Guards that I was a "classist." Not entirely sure of what they had in mind, I said "indeed I am a classicist." They seemed confused with this response, albeit coming from a working class background, I found it odd that upper middle class kids from wealthy homes would be suggesting I am a defender of a privileged class.

To my surprise the deans responded to student activism with complacency and in some instances sympathy, "At least these kids are engaged," noted a colleague from the School of the Arts. I would ask "engaged in what?" Answers were never readily apparent.

From what I could discern at Deans' meetings, a weekly council of deans and university officers including the president, the prevailing sentiment was "no trouble on my watch." When I raised the issue of politicization and its consequences for academic integrity, a fellow dean said, "It's too far gone. There isn't much that we can do."

This was a position consistent with every other issue addressed by the deans. When I suggested to a decanal friend that these meetings were a waste of time since so little gets done, he nodded and replied, "Yes, that's why I think they are necessary. This is the one time during the week I can daydream and not worry that I'm missing something important." That comment hit home.

After numerous meetings in which little if anything was accomplished, the president asked if there were any matter that should be raised for the good of the order. Summoning my pent up frustration with previous meetings, I said, "the discussion at these meetings is comparable to board meetings at a corporation. We discuss financial matters abstractly but never discuss educational issues." There was a pregnant moment of silence. The president looked at me with a steely gaze and said, "Any other comments?" The meeting adjourned; I had learned yet another lesson.

It wasn't the only lesson I learned at these meetings. Arguably the most important issue deans had to decide was the tuition rate for the following year. The university's vice president for financial affairs came well armed with statistics on cost and revenue projection. Since NYU is a private university charging tuition five times what most public institutions do, I suggested an examination of demand elasticity; i.e., would higher tuition rates reduce student attendance. Various components were put into a matrix that addressed this question. However, despite all the analysis, one issue dominated the tuition decision: Yale's anticipated tuition rate. Since NYU fashioned itself as Yale on the Square, the tuition at the institution NYU aspired to be trumped all other arguments, even those deemed most logical.

Curiously, logic was often in short supply at these meetings. On another occasion one dean noted that classroom space in the Main Building was limited during the hours of 6 to 8 PM from Monday through Thursday. Classrooms were allocated based on seniority with the older schools having the preponderance of spaces. Since I was representing a new college, rooms in the Main Building at the peak demand hours were unavailable to me. Since I considered this arrangement unfair and unreasonable, I proposed a simple solution—a pricing system. Those deans who believed they could fill classrooms might pay a premium for these spaces, thereby rationalizing the allocational arrangement. In addition, I noted, that since classrooms are empty on Fridays (every professor believes he is entitled to a three day weekend), spaces in the Main Building should not be taxed at all on Fridays—free space, as it were.

Although I was proud of my simple plan, it had the effect of a nuclear explosion. Those deans privileged to have spaces allocated, even when the rooms were half empty, would not rescind a special arrangement. That was a tough nut to crack, but virtually a bagatelle compared to the response of faculty members who, after learning that a dean was proposing or encouraging Friday classes, were prepared to organize an auto de fé for me in Washington Square Park. I can still hear the ringing in my ears from disgruntled colleagues, many of whom refused to talk to me again. Needless to say, this London plan was dropped like a hot potato never to be heard from again.

I learned that logic and special interests may diverge but special interests, i.e., faculty interests, always prevail. Let me cite another case in point: There was a time in the seventies when the faculties decided that all three-point courses in the university should be four-point courses. An argument was made that there must be additional assignments and a rigorous program to sustain the change. I realized it was a calculated effort to reduce the faculty teaching load since most faculty members prefer free time to classroom time—a perfectly understandable condition. During deliberations over this matter, I was a minority of one insisting that it was irresponsible to eliminate a quarter of one's undergraduate education. But despite my protestations about the injury to the accumulated knowledge of students, my minority status remained unaltered among my professional colleagues.

At some point, this minority position seemed suitable for me. By dint of my decanal status I had a position on the University Senate. Invariably the vote on almost every issue was seventy-seven to one. Since a voice vote, would drown out my dissent, I usually asked for a roll call vote which the president reluctantly accepted.

At one meeting there was a discussion and subsequent proposal to prevent the Navy from recruiting on campus because of its avowed stance against homosexuals. Members of the gay community, who were well represented in this university body, were particularly adamant about this position arguing that the principle in this case, namely discrimination, had to be recognized and condemned. I argued that there was another principle at stake, namely the maintenance of an open campus, even for those with whom many disagree. The vote was taken and, as I expected, I lost seventy-seven to one.

At the time I not only served on the NYU Senate, I served as a board member at the Center for Naval Analysis, a federally funded center that engaged in strategic thinking for the U.S. Navy. Since it was a federal institution, the secretary of the Navy, at the time John Lehman, served as the chairman. Soon after the NYU Senate vote, the center had a board meeting and I told John about the university's decision. He replied angrily; "That cannot happen." "Alas," I noted, "it did happen." "No you don't understand. The U.S. Navy provides $10 million in basic research funds for the university's Courant Institute for Mathematics and Computer Science. If the university doesn't want our recruiters, I guess it doesn't want our money either." Sensing an opportunity to hoist these self-satisfied "idealists" by their own petard, I suggested that the Secretary say that to the president of the university.

A few days after John Lehman spoke to the university president, I received word that an emergency meeting of the Senate was being called. A smile crossed my face since I had a strong suspicion why this meeting was organized. The president with the utmost sincerity said, "We are facing a serious crisis. Despite a recent vote based on the principle that homosexuals should not be denied their place in any institution in this society, I have discovered that our thoughtful action imperiled the welfare of one of this institution's finest programs, the Courant Institute. If we stand by our position, we will lose $10 million of Navy support and threaten the existence of the mathematics program. Therefore I am calling on you to vote again and take an action different from your previous vote."

I couldn't resist. "Mr. President," I said, "weren't we asked to vote on the basis of principle. Are you now telling us that principles have a price tag and are subject to manipulation?" I could see the anger building in the president's face. Without responding to me, he noted that if there aren't any more questions or comments he would call for a vote. Yes, you guessed it, the vote was seventy-seven to one. This time I was on the other side in what I can only describe as the most delicious moment in my thirty-eight years at NYU.

Needless to say, there were many moment of abject frustration. One of the most notable was the orientation session for first year students (political correctness forbids me from saying freshmen). There were many extraordinary events planned by the Student Affairs Office, including attendance at a baseball games, Broadway shows, museum visits, etc. But then there were the "re-education programs," the introduction to the university's political agenda.

A member of the office of transgender and gay orientation would address the assembled body of seventeen- and eighteen-year-olds by asking, "Are any of you confused about your sexuality?" Now unless I am hopelessly antediluvian, my guess is most teenagers are confused since most are not yet sexually active. This spokesman, however, had an agenda. "Well if you're confused," he noted, "please come to our office for consultation."

To gild the lily (no pun intended) there were spokesmen from various homosexual groups representing every ethnic and religious group on campus, i.e. Puerto Rican homosexuals, Jewish homosexuals, African American homosexuals, etc., that addressed the student body. Curiously omitted was a heterosexual group. Presumably, heteros aren't sexually confused.

That isn't the end of what I believe was an absurd exercise in deep-seated propagandistic purpose. At the end of the school year the university's president, seated with the deans of the various colleges, would confer service awards. To my dismay the president would give an award to the Puerto Rican homosexuals' organization for recruiting eleven new members. Everyone in attendance would applaud as if this were an achievement comparable to obtaining a Phi Beta Kappa key.

Since I was obliged to participate, I sat there stone-faced, convinced that I had wandered into a strange new world where my views had been turned on their head. After the first year of my participation, I scheduled an illness whenever the service award ceremony was held. In my case, not seeing was not believing. My eyes and ears had a jarring effect on my sensibility. And as I saw it, a respite from the absurd was definitely warranted.

There was no doubt I was out of place in university life, a square peg in a round hole. However, I was proud of the fact I was the first member of my family to graduate from college. And obtaining a PhD and having the "elevated" status of dean was a source of pride for my parents. Both Mom and Dad were obliged to start working at an early age. My dad enrolled at City College, but had to drop out so he could support his mother and brother (his father was an absentee dad).

So when I invited them for lunch at the university's faculty lounge, it was a big deal. Dressed to the nines, they paraded into this setting expecting professors to be as well dressed as they were. Of course, that wasn't the case. My mom said "these people look like unmade beds. Don't they realize they are models for youngsters." That argument had a searing effect. She's right, I thought.

The next day I sent a memo to faculty members saying that jeans and t-shirts are no longer acceptable attire in the classroom. I noted further that if the professoriate didn't have a suit or a dress, I would buy one. Two days after my missive was sent, I received a call from the president. Apparently my faculty members complained that I was dictatorial and that a dress code should not be imposed on them.

Realizing this matter probably deserved consultation, I called for a faculty meeting at which the matter was discussed. Despite seeming reluctance, there was consensus that minimal standards of acceptable attire were necessary. A self-evident standard was achieved, albeit one that would never have satisfied my mother.

I sometimes felt that my mother, who was a high school dropout, had a far better sense of how the world worked than most of my faculty colleagues. There was one incident that seemingly reinforced that judgment.

In the heat of revolutionary sentiment on campus almost every core requirement for graduation was abandoned. Students simply accumulated credits of almost any kind, and that met a graduation standard. Science and math requirements were deposited on the ash heap of history. Concerned that the degree had been so diluted by incremental concessions to radicals, the deans proposed an introductory course that would be required of all students. It was called Critical Thinking. Surely they thought students in any discipline should be able to think critically, a judgment that was impossible to oppose. How you get from innocence to sophistication or from a lack of judgment to critical judgment wasn't seriously entertained.

So this grand experiment began with incoming students. On one occasion, I was in the corridor of the Main Building when I heard an instructor say to his class "our first session in critical thinking will be the examination of a world that runs out of fossil fuels. What do you think should be done?" One student said we can get new energy sources by going to the moon. No one bothered to ask him about the energy necessary to reach the moon. Another said we can harness the energy of the sun, albeit how we apply solar energy and batteries wasn't clear.

The more I heard, the more it was obvious that this was an exercise in the exchange of ignorant opinion. Since these students knew almost nothing about the laws of supply and demand, pricing never entered the discussion. Since they hadn't taken a course in physics and knew nothing about the conservation of energy, they could not conceive of the idea you cannot run out of energy, even if fossil fuels might be reduced. Since they knew nothing about history, they weren't prepared to discuss commodity shortages in the past.

In other words, the lofty ideal of critical thinking could not be obtained until students know something. One cannot think critically until there is a knowledge base on which to rely. Without this base, opinions are generally ignorant, a form of mental masturbation. Surely my mother could have told that to my decanal colleagues, but they wouldn't have listened and, after all, they know it all.

Chapter Six

What Really Matters

From the very inception of the Gallatin School, I believed that the delivery system might by experimental even if the curriculum remained traditional. I believed as well that cross school registration could enhance the educational experience and that independent study—if carefully monitored—might be a desirable enhancement for students. However, I did not accept the proposition that standards should be modified or that grades were unimportant.

Since the promise I made to the president was that students in my program will have read great books before they graduate, I was obliged to prepare a list of great books as the central requirement to the program. While there will always be a debate about book selection, why *X* as opposed to *Y*, the books selected have passed the test of time. As I see it, there were few surprises. the Bible, Melville, Shakespeare, Sophocles, Aeschylus. Hobbes, Euripides, Homer, Plato, Chaucer, Aristotle, Milton, Tolstoy, Dostoyevsky, Machiavelli, Marx, Dante, Freud, Nietzsche, Darwin, Locke, Austen, Rousseau, Bronte, Cervantes, Trollope, Dickens, et al (this is not a complete list). There was a mix of philosophy, literature and social theory. Although I have strong political convictions, my bias didn't enter into this list of eighty-seven books. Mine was an Arnoldian decision simply to identify the best that is known and thought. The "list," as it became known, was the foundation of the program.

Not only were students expected to read these texts and take seminars on the books, but when they were eligible for graduation demonstrate they were expected to conversant with the themes. At these oral exams, three faculty members would interrogate candidates about their general knowledge of the texts. Students weren't asked to comment on Canto 54 of Dante's *Inferno*, but they were expected to explain Dante's position in this epic poem. Yes, I could say that students graduating from the Gallatin School had read great books.

Not all my students passed this exam. Those who didn't take the assignment seriously had to repeat the experience after taking a semester off. Some regarded the assignment as arbitrary. And others complained to the administration about this "artificial" hurdle for graduation, but I was intractable. If you weren't ready for this assignment, you weren't ready for the Gallatin School. In the more than two decades I administered this program, this list remained intact. Politics were not part of the equation and those who took the exam and passed often remarked that it was a highlight of their undergraduate education.

Yet it is also true that nothing remains the same in higher education. One of my decanal successors left the list unchanged. But another, who readily admitted she had another agenda, started to tinker with it. "What is a great book?" she asked. She answered her own question by arguing my list represented a tradition bound, politically conservative agenda. As a consequence, she believed Franz Fanon, Shulamith Firestone and Toni Morrison, among others, should be on the list for "balance" (her word). While I would not object to students reading these authors, I was persuaded their addition to the list diluted the meaning of the program and was an intentional political act. Although I was long gone from the School, I wrote a letter to the dean about the changes claiming her selections altered the meaning of a great books program.

To my surprise a reporter at the *New York Times* got wind of the controversy and decided to interview us together. The reporter eager for controversy started the discussion by noting we had different conceptions of "experimental education." Indeed we had. I explained how my list was conceived and why the authors selected stood the test of time. My successor indicated all things change and the list should be more representative of feminist impulses, racial concerns, and contemporary politics. I countered by noting these ideas are actually incorporated into the original list. Moreover, the quality of the new additions was, in my opinion, not commensurate with other authors on the list. At this point she noted, in a statement I will never forget that, "It is more important for students to read Toni Morrison than Shakespeare." Now I have nothing against Ms. Morrison who is widely regarded as a superior novelist. But "superior to Shakespeare?" I sat there shaking my head. What happened to the standard I believe in and attempted to impress on the school? It was strange, but I left that interview shaking my head.

On reflection, I responded like a disgruntled parent. My child was being spoiled by a surrogate parent. Even though the umbilical chord was cut, I felt some intervention was necessary, even if it were little more than a defense of my reputation and the mission of the school. But this effort was hopeless; affirmative action assailed the Gallatin list, and I was disheartened. It seemed that the wave of radical sentiment had penetrated every crevice of university life. I tried to point out that radical sentiment could be found in Marx, Rousseau, Voltaire, among others. Yet with a cavalier gesture of dismissal, these authors were put in the box of dead, white, European males. It wasn't merely radicalism that prevailed, but philistinism masquerading as radical thought.

Having cogitated about this situation, I decided to write a letter to the president of the university. I explained with all the passion I felt why this change in the list violated the mission of the school and challenged my efforts. To demonstrate my seriousness about the matter, I asked him to remove my portrait, which hangs in the school as a tribute to my role as founder. As you might guess, I never received reply, not even acknowledgment. "No trouble on my watch" was not merely a slogan, it was the modus operandi of the president. Why should the president take a stand on a matter that didn't personally affect him? After all, London is no longer affiliated with the school. Why should he be sticking his nose into the matter? Principle be damned.

As a consequence, the Gallatin School was formally radicalized. Moreover, to make sure my influence would be marginalized, the history of the school's founding was altered suggesting that faculty members I hired had actually launched the institution. This had the affect of writing me out of the history, a device that came right out of the Soviet encyclopedia. And it superordinated the role of faculty members who employed this historical revisionism to secure tenure, a status that their limited scholarship did not warrant.

This episode represented my last big lesson. No longer was I Don Quixote, now I was the Man in the Gray Flannel Suit who disappeared into the university shadows. Sure, I harbored some resentment, but that soon passed. I could recall with fondness building a school, defending its mission and educating literally thousands who passed through its doors. Occasionally I run into one of those students who remind me that the great books list as originally conceived had a profound influence on his life. That always brings a smile to my lips, albeit I can never be sure if these graduates are referring to the old or the altered book list.

Chapter Seven

Letter to a Student

Suppose you are high school student about to enter Columbia College or NYU's College of Arts and Science, what should you know? What can a former dean and faculty member tell you? I've thought about this a great deal and here is my advice.

Think of university life as a strange new world with exotic flora and fauna. You have the opportunity to touch, taste and experience it all. Since it is new and exotic, you have to overcome the fear factor, but, of course, your classmates are in the same position, although most seem more confident than you.

This is also a four year hiatus from responsibility. You should think of classes as a catalyst for formal reading. If a subject excites you, think big. Identify the major books in that discipline and read every one of them. You don't have to be an A student to be a serious student. The evening bull session with friends is the time to try out what you've read. See if you can explain complicated ideas. Don't be afraid to gamble with your thoughts. After all, you're talking to friends.

Identify one, maybe two, professors, who could serve as a guide. Volunteer for a research project this professor is working on. Professors love to have free labor.

Above all remain a skeptic. Don't accept professorial opinion at face value. "What is the evidence for that claim?" is a good way to challenge professors and a helpful way for you to learn.

Join a team. I recently read in *The American*[1] that people who played sports in high school and college earn higher incomes in adulthood than those who did not play on a team. The theory, borne out by my experience, is that competition in sports prepares people for competition in life and makes them better suited for the vicissitudes in a free market. It also helps people to deal with failure, an unavoidable condition on the basketball court and in business. The true test of character is being able to cope with loss.

Of course, even if you are a gifted athlete, keep your priorities in order. The average eighteen-year-old will start to see his God-given talents diminish in his thirties. Those playing division I sports are sometimes described as student athletes, but in big-time college sports coaches care about the three-point shot, not your cumulative average. Coach (a definite article is never is never used for coaches) doesn't usually concern himself with your understanding of Thomas Hobbes, he wants to know if you've been lifting weights and can generate victories that enhance his reputation and the size of his next contract.

Remember that deans and most administrators want to help you. After all, you pay their salaries. They have a stake in seeing you succeed. Someday you may even be an alumnus making contributions to alma mater. You may have to overcome a natural reluctance to reach out, but once you do, encounters will be relatively easy.

It is also important to recognize the difference that sometimes arises between a grade and a learning experience. In an era of soft or undifferentiated grades, most students do well. In fact, I could not distinguish between the honor roll and the student roster in the Gallatin School. It was as if every student was above average. Your peers will say you must get outstanding grades to get into the best law schools or medical schools. This is a trope that bears little relationship to reality. Standardized tests mean more than grades since admissions officers have generally discounted the veracity of grades. As I see it, the important thing is to learn something of value, to develop skills and to see the world with fresh perspectives. "Educate" is a reflexive verb, one educates oneself, notwithstanding help along the learning path. Use this college experience as if you were Columbus about to enter the New World.

If you are about to graduate, think of the commencement exercise as an extended address by Fidel Castro. Not only is it usually a soporific experience, but it is invariably advice offered by left-wing ideologies. At NYU, for example, Representative Charles Rangel, a tax cheat who has several rent controlled apartments, received on honorary degree for reasons that eluded me other than the fact he is an African American.

Last, a university is a vast nest that protects you from the demands of everyday life. Enjoy that comfortable life through the joys of study and contemplation. Years later you will look back and recall the opportunities that you were given. Don't suffer regrets by drinking your way through four years as an undergraduate. Of course, it has been said that education is wasted on the young. But this is one of those bromides that can be overcome. The choice is yours.

NOTE

1. Scott Ganz and Kevin Hassett, "Field of Dreams," *The American*, May/June, 2008.

Chapter Eight

The Zeitgeist Rings My Home Number

I woke up to the sounds of a megaphone in 1970. It was the day President Nixon had American forces attack Cambodia; a day the war spread from Vietnam to a contiguous nation because the president refused to allow the enemy a sanctuary. But what I heard from that megaphone were chants that it is time to declare war against America.

My apartment house, which abutted Washington Square Park, was ringed with demonstrators. This was street theater that surpassed anything I had previously experienced in what I have called the "overheated decade."

As soon as I reached my office that day, I received word that a special faculty meeting had been called for that very morning. The faculty, sharing a distaste for the war, was in high dungeon. One of my colleagues, who is normally sensible on the issues, said, "Nixon has gone too far. We must act." What we should do, however, was not immediately apparent.

The one thing faculty members can do is deliver speeches. People rose to express their indignation. One faculty member argued that we should go to Washington and take our government back. Who we are taking it from wasn't clear, but clarity was unnecessary at that time. This was the moment to vent.

After dozens of repetitive speeches, someone suggested that the faculty propose the closing of the university as a period of contemplation and a time when students should be permitted to go to Washington to demonstrate. In this environment there was a certain logic to the proposal, which became a motion, but I wasn't buying it.

Before the vote was taken, the dean asked if there were comments pro and con on the matter. Despite some reluctance to speak out on the subject, since I represented a distinctly different posture, I rose to speak. Without mentioning the fact that I was opposed to the Vietnam War before I left for Australia, but returned believing American military presence in Asia was necessary to preserve area stability, I proceeded to argue that the maintenance of an open university was essential for the well-being of the academic enterprise. Closing the university to satisfy partisans of one position, whatever the position might be, would establish a dangerous precedent. Moreover, by encouraging this time-off for students to demonstrate, the university was establishing itself as an advocate of political action, a view not unlike what students in South America were encouraged to do.

Recognizing it as a minority opinion, I delivered my speech with dispassion. But to my surprise, when the vote was taken my side won a narrow victory. NYU would remain open, or so I thought.

In the ensuing days, violence—or should I say the threat of violence—increased. A bomb was installed in a science lab, but fortunately it was discovered and dismantled .There were other threats as well, threats that probably forced the hand of the president who decided to suspend classes and close the university despite the faculty vote.

My stance was different. Since the faculty voted to remain open, I thought the president had an obligation to deploy the university's security staff to maintain order and keep the buildings open. When asked to revote, I asked sarcastically, "Do we vote until we get it right?" I guess that was the case since the faculty did not support my opinion in this matter.

However, filled with self righteousness (a quality I've subsequently lamented), I decided to hold my classes relying on the decision in the first vote. I send a telegram (this was 1970) to every student notifying each one that my classes would be held and their attendance was strongly encouraged.

The demonstrators also got wind of my decision. As I marched into the Main Building with students at my side, I had to pass a cordon of detractors who threw eggs and tomatoes at me. When one of these youngsters attempted to block my path, I pushed him aside as cries of "fascist" filled the corridors of the first floor. While I lectured bullhorns blared in an effort to disrupt the class. But I was adamant, perhaps foolish. I wasn't going to let these self appointed apostles of political correctness determine my posture.

Years later, I met one of the students in that class who said she could scarcely recall anything that happened in her four years at NYU, but she would never forget the events on that fateful day in 1970. I found that quite gratifying, even though the ultimate effect of my action on university life was insignificant.

I never thought of myself as an iconoclast, but it did seem odd that the university faculty appeared to be a herd of independent thinkers. So self assured were they, that an opinion that didn't fit the prevailing sentiment was either ignored or driven from polite discourse. I often wondered what happened to the idea of unfettered conversation, of the respectful exchange of opinion.

It was clearly disappearing, and I wasn't the only person who observed this condition.

One distinguished faculty member in the sciences took the time to send me a note which, through deciphering, seemed to be commending me for my actions. However, the handwriting was so small it was impossible to read. I called him to express my gratitude, but asked why he didn't type the note or have his secretary do so since it was indecipherable. His reply was very revealing: "I didn't want anyone to know I agree with you." So much for a display of faculty courage.

Of course there were rarely faculty members who did agree with me, albeit that was a condition to which I became accustomed.

In 1984, the faculty of Arts and Science at NYU approved a "minor" in peace studies with only one dissent in the faculty vote. This new minor was expected to evolve into an academic major. As I saw it, this was an academic liberal's effort to impose his brand of peace on an unwary student population.

The program was run by a psychologist who maintained that "the urgent war-peace issue of our time . . . must be addressed." The core of the program was a two-credit course, "Nuclear War and Its Prevention." He argued he was eager to promote diverse thinking, not indoctrination. However, an original founder of the program, a physicist, belied this dispassion with his claim that the timing is "very important especially since the administration wants to go ahead with the Star Wars project . . . and devote millions of dollars to it."

It is worth asking why the assignments don't include the works of Herman Kahn, Colin Gray and Robert Jastrow, respected thinkers on nuclear arms. Is Jonathan Schell, author of *The Fate of the Earth*, the only panjandrum of nuclear strategy? Is the Star Wars Strategic Defense Initiative to be viewed solely as an escalation in the arms race? Is it appropriate for a peace program to espouse the view that only by defeating an antimissile strategy can peace be preserved?

Once again, the canons of scholarship were ignored by true believers. In this case, peace studies didn't make the slightest gesture to opposing viewpoints. It is a "discipline" imperialized by a psychologist. Is a psychologist with no background in military affairs really competent to teach such a course?

The driving interest of "peace scholars"—the one that awakened the sensibilities in the first place—was student activism. Mobilizing student support for the scholars' peace agenda was unstated, but seemed the real goal in this and other such programs. Peace programs, or those euphemistically called programs in conflict resolution, are the battleground for academic opinion makers. These are scholars who intended to win a war for the minds of students who will be pressed into the service of a controversy they don't entirely understand.

In NYU's Nuclear War and Its Prevention course, three readings were required: Roger Molander, *Nuclear War, What's in it For You*; Burns Weston (editor), *Toward Nuclear Disarmament and Global Security*"; and Carl Sagan, "Nuclear War and Climactic Catastrophe" (which appeared in *Foreign Affairs* in 1983). The deck could scarcely be stacked more completely. Moreover, this was done without the slightest embarrassment, apparently without concern for fair play. The instructor, in my view, made it perfectly clear that it is not scholarship that is sought, but rather faithful congregants.

There have been similar movements in higher education. Since most academics are inclined to turn the other cheek, these programs become institutionalized. Some die of noninterest. But this one threatened to spill over into the political arena, where half-educated students filled with moral indignation become a lobbying group for a particular brand of peace crusade.

It wasn't difficult to see what was happening. Academic conciliators have found allies in their students. These "academic" programs were really designed to battle with the Strategic Defense Initiative, the MX missile and any other strategic system introduced by the Reagan Administration.

Not only did I express my views forthrightly, but I expressed them on the pages of the *New York Times*. The article was published on a Tuesday, and the deans' meeting was held the following day. As I entered the president's conference room to greet my decanal colleagues, I could sense the coolness in the air. It didn't take long for the dean of the business school to upbraid me for violating a confidence. This was a rather odd comment since the program was to be listed in the university catalogue for anyone to read. My self-appointed critic also noted that it was inappropriate for a dean to criticize university programs in so public a manner. I pointed out that since approval was nearly unanimous, the only way to get attention for another view was publishing this article. He remained unpersuaded and I remained defiant.

The psychologist in charge of the peace studies program proceeded to attack me on the pages of the university newspaper, but the editor gave me an opportunity to respond which I was delighted to do. Like most university tempests this one passed, so too did the interest in peace studies, which like so many other faddist disciplines was interred only to be disinterred when another group of psychologists finds a way to save mankind.

Inventing disciplines is, I've discovered, an academic pastime. When feminist studies was first introduced, also as a minor, I asked what might be included in the curriculum. I assumed students would read Jane Austen, Charlotte Bronte and George Eliot. But I was told what is truly important is self expression. Women, suffocated by male oppression, had to vent, to speak out. How one evaluated this venting was somewhat obscure.

Like most new disciplines the expectation is that in time it would be a "major." And once that goal was achieved, it might even become a graduate program. Presumably, it would produce graduates who would seek positions espousing the methods and expressiveness the program encouraged. Feminist studies would ultimately be represented in the councils of the major scholarly organizations, e.g., the feminist side of American historiography through the American Historical Association (AHA). Finally the feminists, in order to meet the requirement for publication, must start a journal and alas, they did, *Clitoral Hermaneutics* (no I didn't make this up).

Considering the fact that faculty members in this discipline will seek and receive tenure and, on top of that, the department will accommodate students with an interest in venting (preparation for this exercise isn't necessary), you begin to understand how difficult it is to undo this academic superstructure once it is established.

If one really wanted to recognize the absurd dimensions of higher education there is no need to look further than the so called new disciplines, which, as it turns out, are usually new but rarely disciplines. This was a pet peeve of mine. I am not suggesting that new knowledge doesn't exist. On the contrary, computer development and scientific breakthroughs have had a profound influence on science and math courses. I am referring to the trivial, to the fads, to the make-believe disciplines that diminish the seriousness of the academic enterprise. How far in an unwholesome direction curriculum reform has gone I didn't fully recognize until I resigned as dean in 2003.

Chapter Nine

Challenging the Academic Orthodoxy

In the mid-1980s when it was clear a left-wing orthodoxy had taken root in the Academy, three of my colleagues, Peter Shaw, Barry Gross, and Steve Balch, decided that we should organize a faculty group to counter what we regarded as a pernicious trend. Steve became the president of what we at first called the Campus Coalition for Democracy, but later became the National Association of Scholars. I was to become the organization's first chairman.

Our goal was clear: the revival of a university environment in which the free and open exchange of opinion was encouraged. Despite journalistic views to the contrary, early members were liberals—not conservatives—distressed by the increasingly narrow and politicized view of academic life. There was also a side bar to our concerns: we wanted to encourage a core curriculum, one that gave students the requisite background for the pursuit of knowledge.

It was apparent that most parents who spend $50,000 a year to send their children to prestigious private colleges across the country and state legislators who subsidize students to the tune of $15,000 a year in public colleges assume that graduates of our institutions of higher learning have some acquaintance with mathematical principles; historical, philosophical, and literary interpretation; a grasp of science; and perhaps some exposure to great artistic pursuits. While there was an empirical basis for these assumptions during much of the last century, it is increasingly difficult to justify such claims today.

A recent study by the National Association of Scholars[1] (NAS), *The Dissolution of General Education: 1914–1993* (September 30, 1996), postulates that a "radical transformation" has taken place in higher education in which basic survey courses have been purged from the curriculum. To test this hypothesis, NAS researchers examined the requirement for a bachelor of arts degree at fifty of the top-ranked institutions in the nation. What the study demonstrates is what many academics have long suspected: the nation's leading institutions have abandoned the core academic requirements once considered the essence of a sound curriculum and the basis for a democratic society.

Overall, the study found that structured course requirements were the norm in 1914, 1939, and 1964; but by 1993 these requirements had declined precipitously. Moreover, graduation requirements incorporating general education courses dropped significantly as well. There are now fewer mandatory courses, fewer clusters, fewer courses with prerequisites and longer completion time than was the case heretofore. In addition, the study indicated that today's students at leading colleges are not held to the exacting standards that once prevailed in the academy. For example, more than 50 percent of the schools in the study demanded a thesis or comprehensive examination as a requirement for a baccalaureate degree between 1939 and 1964. By 1993, only 12 percent of the institutions in the study maintained this requirement.

With their roots firmly planted in the soil of the 1960s, academics willingly, or in some cases reluctantly, accepted the proposition advocated by radical students that judgments could not be made about what should and should not be studied. Alas, the *cri de Coeur* from the barricades for student choice became official policy less than a decade later.

Commitment to structured general education requirements and rigorous standards for the completion of a degree have, as the NAS study demonstrated, been vitiated. For some, participatory democracy has had a natural and understandable effect on the curriculum. As Sidney Hook, Paul Kurtz, and Miro Todorvich reported in *The Philosophy of the Curriculum: The Need for General Education*[2], a student at a Washington Square College meeting in the 1960 said, "the intrinsic value or interest of a subject isn't enough to justify prescribing it. Every subject has intrinsic value. If education is to be effective and relevant, it must be related to the personal needs of the students. Without us, you have no justification for your being teachers."

Here, in unadorned form, was the challenge of that decade and beyond, a challenge from which most academics have retreated. Some scholars contend that students should have the choice of a college curriculum—not merely the college one wishes to attend—but open-ended opportunities to select any course within the university's catalogue of offerings.

It seems to me there are two conditions this point of view underscores. The first is that an education having any value should be related to individual needs. The second is that students know what they want to study and the consequences of their decisions. After decades in the academy, it seems to me almost axiomatic that propositions one and two are mutually incompatible. What students want is often not what they need, need being defined as that common frame of reference that sustains a liberal society such as ours. To balkanize the curriculum by suggesting students, as unfettered actors on the university stage, can select any course they wish is to admit that professors, with more experience and presumably more knowledge about what to study, should abdicate their responsibility and transfer it to untutored freshmen and sophomores. Yet, mirabile dictu, this is precisely what has been occurring for several decades.

As the NAS study noted, broad exposure to areas of knowledge and the attainment of skills have been declining dramatically since 1964. To cite one example: the percentage of institutions with composition requirements administered by English departments slipped from 86 percent in 1964 to 36 percent in 1993. The present university curriculum has gone very far down the road of student participatory democracy, leaving in its wake a hodgepodge of general education programs and ambiguity about priorities in undergraduate education. As some detractors of the academy point out, the current university curriculum can be analogized to a Chinese menu, e.g., two from column A and three from column B, without any particular pattern or coherence emerging.

Granted, students will ultimately make career decisions and select majors on their own and, granted as well, we have experienced a knowledge explosion. Nevertheless, it is incumbent on professors to identify what is to be studied within our social context. It is not arbitrary and inappropriate for the faculty to say that in its considered judgment there are indispensable courses all students should experience. Surely, curriculum decisions are not entirely one-sided. They unfold from the debate about curriculum that is never ending. But a faculty, as I see it, should not abandon its authority to be at the very center of these decisions.

A former dean and present vice-president for information technology at Middlebury College, Eric Davis argued that it is desirable to have fewer required core courses. "To expect all students to take the same course, read the same books, hear the same lecture, is a format of study that's too rigid and too restrictive for the modern world," he said. What Professor Davis does not say is that the humanities are predicated on an understanding of our common *humanitas*. The humanities are, in fact, based not on the superficial differences that separate us, such as race and ethnicity, but the common bonds of empathy, sorrow, loyalty, love, bravery, and cowardice that unite us.

A culture divorced from its common bonds does not have the amalgam to cohere. When students are unaware of common cultural cues, when the voices of deep human understanding, e.g., Shakespeare, are ignored, when the achievements of Western civilization are derided and subsequently subordinated to the study of other civilizations, then the die for cultural dissolution is cast. I have given lectures with passing reference to phrases rooted in the culture, such as "panglossian," "Achilles' heel," "Alice's rabbit hole," 'the ides of March," and "Hobson's choice." However, to my astonishment, the college students I encountered did not know the meanings. Admittedly, this does not exhaust the range and depth of liberal education, but it is symptomatic, in my judgment, of a shift in cultural understanding.

Lacking perspective, students are often unaware of the disparity between ideals and reality. Without some grounding in the essential works of our civilization, great books if you will, students confuse the possible with the probable. Moreover, even ·the radical sensibility cannot be nourished unless there is some understanding about what one is rebelling against. Education is not existential. Whether we like it or not we are tied organically to the past. To neglect that means that in every course the wheel must be reinvented. Either we recognize the role of higher education as a transmission belt from past to present, or we are caught in a seamless web of enigmas and relativism. John Dewey notwithstanding, I am persuaded Aristotle was right: education should pass on the previous contributions of human thought.

Unfortunately, universities often do not appreciate this role in their mission, albeit most give lip service to the idea of cultural transmission. A curious condition of inventiveness without background has insinuated itself into much of what passes for higher education. Perhaps the following illustration makes this point, although I do not pretend generalizations can be derived from a sample of one, and I realize that even courses grounded in tradition can be taught poorly and have little value.

A student interested in playwriting came to see me about his course of study. Since he expressed an interest in contemporary drama, I asked if he had read Bertolt Brecht, Harold Pinter, or Jerzy Grotowski. "Oh man," he exclaimed, "I don't even know those dudes." 'Well," I replied, "don't you think you should at least read other playwrights?" "Oh no," he proclaimed, "that would only screw up my head. I've got to keep myself open for new experiences." Of one thing I am sure: his head is very open. While this student may represent an extreme example, he is not atypical of those who contend that freedom translates into a lack of regimen and few constraints. Apparently many soi-disant artists in the academy have not read André Gide, who wrote: "Art is born of discipline and dies of freedom."

Sidney Hook, in *The Paradoxes of Freedom*[3], argued that a freedom cult can develop an orthodoxy so rigid it inhibits the very action it was designed to promote. How, it might be asked, can students write novels when they have not read novels? How can students measure results in an experiment if they haven't studied basic math? How can students criticize Western civilization when they haven't been exposed to the canon of Western thought? Indeed, how can professors claim to have educated their students when course selection is largely arbitrary and professors have lost confidence in their ability to define the bachelor's degree?

Critics of a highly structured curriculum are right to contend that individuals learn at different paces and with different aptitudes. But I disagree that autonomy of student choice flows from these assumptions. There is material that all students should know, even if they learn it at their own pace and under conditions consistent with their readiness to learn. Not everyone should read Shakespeare as a first-year college student, but every college graduate should have read some Shakespeare. What does a college education mean without exposure to Shakespeare, Plato, Aristotle, Dante, Homer, Milton, and Tolstoy, to cite only a few examples from my great books list. For graduates who have not been exposed to great works, there is only a discredited degree, one that suggests that the students' years in an institution of higher learning may have left no significant impression.

Napoleon once said, "A form of government that is not the result of a long sequence of shared experiences, efforts, and endeavors can never take root." So it is with the relationship between society and university education. Without a shared experience, citizens are open to any claim and stand naked in the public square, unable to defend what they believe or deny what they do not.

Dr. Johnson pointed out that, "Teaching a horse how to count doesn't make him a mathematician." George Bernard Shaw once said, 'Taking an ass around the world doesn't make him a horse." The study of the humanities does not necessarily lead to humanism. And reading philosophy does not necessarily mean one will lead a successful life. But learning how to count is the basis for math, experience can be a great teacher, the study of the humanities can awaken insight about oneself and others and philosophy can pose the questions from which a good life is derived.

If a university education loses sight of its core and if faculty members retreat before the "nonnegotiable" demand for student freedom, then the university as we have known it and on which our society depends, will be an institution marginalized by its unwillingness to uphold the best that is known and written. As I see it, the NAS study represents a wake-up call for the academy. There is still time to save our universities, but only if academics realize how poorly the student body is being served with the present pick-your-own-courses curriculum.

NOTES

1. NAS is an organization of professors designed to promote the free and open exchange of opinion on campus.
2. Prometheus Books, Buffalo, NY, 1975.
3. University of California Press, Berkley, CA, 1962.

Chapter Ten

The Tenure Trap

While tenure is one of those sacred Cows in higher education, I soon discovered it has more down- than upside. There isn't any question that when an ideological crusade occurs as was the case with McCarthyism in the fifties, tenure is a valuable shield against unfair charges. Surely, the imposition of an ideology from the left or the right hasn't any place in the Academy. Nevertheless, a leftist view began to penetrate the walls of Ivy in the late sixties and is firmly ensconced today. As a consequence, tenure now protects ideologies it was designed to oppose. No one to my knowledge ousts a professor for his views no matter how radical they may be and no matter how much he proselytizes. Some might argue that Ward Churchill was denied his position at the University of Colorado because he said "Little Eichmanns were killed on 9/11." However offensive that comment might have been, he was fired for misrepresenting himself, plagiarizing his dissertation, and lying about his résumé. Moreover, the courts subsequently decided that his position should be restored (I regard this decision as thoroughly misguided).

When I founded the Gallatin School at NYU, I vowed to keep tenure bound and under lock and key. Having seen professors barely capable of lucid commentary reading from yellowing lecture notes that had not been altered in twenty years, I admit that I have had a jaded position on tenure. Tenure protected them from unemployment, and correspondingly, forced marginal instruction on students. I've often called the university tenured-professor arrangement the best welfare system in America. That is only a slight exaggeration. However, my desire to change the Gallatin program into the Gallatin School required approval of the University Senate. Faculty members, who reflexively defend tenure for personal reasons, will fight vigorously against anyone who challenges this system. I had a choice, alas a Hobson's choice, either abandon my determination to oppose tenure or put Gallatin in the position of not gaining the status of a college. Since I regarded Gallatin as my creation, I could not jeopardize its institutional status. Tenure became reality in the newly created school as I succumbed to the pressure, but I still remain convinced it was the wrong decision.

I also soon learned that the tenure process controlled by other tenured professors can easily be transformed into a political litmus test. Having selected instructors without regard to their politics, I found that those who were first considered for this status all shared a left-liberal orientation. No surprise there. However, since this class of tenured faculty members determine who is next to receive tenure, political matters were elevated in importance, even though a vocal assertion of politics as a criterion was never made.

One faculty member on the tenure track had a reputation as a conservative. She wrote for conservative journals and wrote persuasively. Having seen her teach, I was convinced she was the most talented instructor in the school. The tenure committee, however, argued that she wasn't "collegial." This, of course, was a code word for not being on the same political frequency as the others. Her tenure was denied and I lost an instructor I very much admired.

For faculty members, tenure guarantees lifetime employment. Unless you commit a felony or rape students, job security will be intact. Where in the economy are positions guaranteed like this? It is an arrangement made in hell for administrators who are often obliged to defend marginal instructors.

To top it off, tenure encourages arrogance and self-importance. After all, tenured faculty members do not care about challenges. Despite this fact, many faculties are unionized, that is a strange and complicated condition since the faculty really runs the institution. Tenure gives them lifetime control, a control administrators will never possess. When a faculty expresses dismay with the way a college is managed, it should be forced to look in the mirror. As Pogo of comic book fame noted: "We have met the enemy and he is us But self-examination is rarely in the cards and tenure militates against it.

As you might guess, I still lament the fact I gave in on this tenure decision. I guess I fell into the trap.

Chapter Eleven

Academic Freedom and Free Speech

It has occurred to me that recent events at Columbia in particular and other universities in general point to a confusion between free speech and academic freedom. As a dean, I noted on several occasions that I would be willing to defend the rights of a flat earth advocate to stand on a soap box and deliver a misguided diatribe stating the earth isn't round. However, I would not give this same individual a chair in the astronomy department. That, in graphic terms, is the difference between free speech and academic freedom.

When the president of Columbia indicates that a professor is free to speak his mind, he ignored the prerequisites and professional requirements associated with academic freedom.

In the 1940 AAUP statement on academic freedom, scholars agreed that the freedom to search for truth (*lehrfreiheit*) and the freedom for students to learn (*lernfreiheit*) were requisite conditions in the academy that insured against totalitarian impulses from without.

Furthermore, the authors of the AAUP recognized that freedom imposes responsibility. Without restraint, faculty freedom could become license, which jeopardized the very legitimacy of the Academy. As a consequence, the authors argued for prudent professional standards, i.e., caution in discussing topics unrelated to one's field of expertise. It was instructive that the statement used the words "accurate," "restraint" and "respect for the opinion of others" in the original text. Professionalism could be defined negatively as in the rejection of an inappropriate display of advocacy, unsustainable political argumentation or propagandizing.

During the 1950s, the so-called McCarthy era, academic freedom was usefully employed as a shield from sometimes irrational political attributions about the professoriate made from without. Standing its ground, the AAUP and others raised the torch of freedom to teach, to engage in research and to learn. Although one might contend there were institutions that faltered in this struggle, on balance, the Academy prevailed over the accusers. Whether the accusers represented a totalitarian impulse as was sometimes suggested during that period was less relevant to the argument than a belief that threats to academic freedom cannot be countenance in any form.

In the late sixties a different challenge to the academy emerged. Some students having been suckled on the milk of participatory democracy and believing themselves to be the handmaidens of a new social order, demanded (usually in nonnegotiable terms) an altered college environment. Rather than the freedom to learn, these students demanded the freedom to reform and restructure the academy. While it is hard to make the argument universities simply conceded to radical student sentiment, it is the case that parietals were abandoned, undifferentiated grades were introduced, faculty evaluations were routinely embraced, electives increased geometrically, students sat on university councils, ethnic-racial-gender related courses forged a prominent place in the curriculum. In the brouhaha, what went unnoticed is that faculties abdicated responsibility to maintain professional standards. The words participatory democracy seared the imagination of professors who often did not have the courage to say the obvious: education is not a democratic condition. When the dust settled, professionalism was tarnished as a concept and a practice.

Many of those students and their sympathizers who carried the flag for participatory democracy in the student demonstrations of the sixties are now tenured professors. Having assumed—correctly it turns out—that internal pressure can reform the academic enterprise, that legitimacy is a slim reed on which to defend institutions of higher learning, these recently tenured professors have converted the academy into a center for reform. The verities of the past are candidates for excision like the abandonment of parietals or other "anachronistic" conditions on campus. Where once universities were cultural transmission belts, now they are launching pads for experimentation. Multiculturalism, semiotics, relativism, radical politics are words pegged into the zeitgeist. What each suggests is an effort to overturn an established truth. For the experimenters there isn't any truth, except the display of power that accounts for the removal of one idea for another. Epistemology itself is viewed as a social construct emerging from control of various disciplines, with control being the essential concept.

Since academic freedom can only be discussed in the context of the university's mission and since that mission has been altered dramatically in the last several decades, academic freedom as a concept had been transformed as well. As a shield from outside intrusion, academic freedom has served the academy well; as a standard for professionalism and the antidote to corrosive ideas and irresponsible behavior, it has been a failure. In fact, the problem with the very idea of contemporary academic freedom is that it concentrates on threats from without that rarely exist and overlooks threats from within that have violently disordered the academic mission.

The Academy legitimately makes a claim to be an imperium in imperio. Within colleges set apart from society, there is a belief in self-regulation. Presumably just as the scholar can resist intervention from the critics, the professoriate can resist pressures from the larger society, a form of collective academic freedom. That reality was recognized with some aberrations throughout this century. But now there is a growing awareness that academic freedom can be used to protect irresponsible behavior, that some faculty members have so redefined the profession that any resemblance between professional behavior in the 1940s and the present is merely coincidental.

Recently a professor of English at the University of Wisconsin, who admits to seducing students, claims that she intentionally sexualizes the classroom in order to reduce barriers between students and instructors. When she was brought up on charges of harassment—a case where harassment charges were warranted—the protective shield of academic freedom was raised and university officials relented, suggesting, in effect, that seduction could be tolerated if the students were no longer in the instructor's class.

Similarly, when charges of irresponsibility were leveled against Professor Leonard Jeffries at the City University of New York, over his lecture on "ice people" and "sun people," in which not a shred of evidence to support his contentions was made, he, in a state of high dungeon, raised the banned of academic freedom. Jeffries was removed from his administrative post since it could not be protected by tenure (a decision subsequently rescinded), but he continued to offer his highly questionable theories to unwary students as a tenure professor of Black Studies.

What might be concluded from this analysis is that academic freedom must be redefined for the present state of the Academy. In the first instance, I would argue that academic freedom must retain its traditional and appropriate meaning as a force to maintain the aims of scholarship and learning unmolested by outside political influence. In the second instance, academic freedom should embody the claims of professionalism, stating in terms far more direct and precise than the 1940 statement what this entails.

In my judgment, it should embody the premise that rational exegesis is the sine qua non of scholarship. Appeals to intuition and other vague mystical formulations should not be as persuasive in an Academy of scholars as evidence. Moreover, propagandizing on behalf of one's favorite cause should be discouraged unless it can be demonstrated that such appeal is consistent with the canons of scholarship. Scholarship and teaching should be distinguished from advocacy and preaching. Behavior one would not countenance outside college walls should not be embraced inside those walls. While I have always been skeptical about a university's ability to instill moral and social virtue, the university should enforce a code of conduct for faculty members and students consistent with the requirements of the larger society. If drug use has specific legal restrictions, to cite one example, the university's stance should conform to society's position. And last, professional standards imply rigorous academic pursuits. When latitudinarians define scholarship as "any learning experience" they undermine the meaning of scholarship. Academic freedom should be a bulwark against faddism, unsubstantiated claims and mere social activism. Responsible professors should say, we do not believe that carrying banners in behalf of a cause warrants academic credit, and they should say as well that flabby exercises unrelated to disciplined reading and research will not receive the protective embrace of academic freedom.

Surely my detractors will find examples that challenge my model of professionalism. But in the end, unless consensus of professionalism is established and well understood by the public, as an intrinsic feature of academic freedom, the precious freedom academics cherish will be imperiled by perceived and real irresponsible behavior. Most people do not think of universities as change agents. They expect a university to be a place where high culture is transmitted, skills and knowledge are conveyed and pure research is encouraged. Within these purposes there is much room for interpretation. When Socrates conceived of a center of learning he recognized that thought experimentation and the free exchange of ideas can be risky, but certainly Socrates did not assume the academic enterprise would be frivolous. It is precisely that frivolity in the present state of higher education that must be resisted so that academic freedom can be retained.

Chapter Twelve

The Hudson Institute as a University in Absentia

My growing dismay with the Academy led to an occupational exploration. In several articles that appeared in *Time* and *Life* magazines, I read about a man who seemed to escape institutional confusion of the kind I was saddled with and became his own institution. His name was Herman Kahn, a human think tank, a nightmare for student radicals, a consultant to the Pentagon, the inspiration for Stanley Kubrick's *Dr. Strangelove* and one of the few people who stood up to the furies of that era without faltering.

In one of my impulsive moments, I wrote to Mr. Kahn imploring him for a meeting. It was a shot in the dark; I never expected a reply. But to my delight, I received an invitation to meet Herman at the Hudson Institute. His charming assistant, having read my letter, said, "You're like all of us here, a disenchanted liberal sick to death of the New Left." I knew then and there I had found a congenial sanctuary.

Although Mr. Kahn spoke in rapid-fire speech, virtually spitting out his words, I gathered that he liked my resume and wanted me to work on a project related to drug abuse in New York. He said that the street price of heroin reveals a great deal about the effectiveness of drug enforcement efforts. A high price suggests supply lines have been compromised; a low price, the opposite. "So," he stated, "as your first assignment buy heroin on the streets of Harlem."

I sat there dumbfounded. Attempting to regain my composure, I said, "You must be kidding. What happens if I'm arrested?" Herman responded by assuring me the police will cooperate. All I could think of was my mother reading in the tabloids that her son has been apprehended for buying heroin. And, yes, I did make the purchase of a bag of heroin on 125th Street. This was quite a dramatic introduction to Herman Kahn and the Hudson Institute.

What I discovered is that Herman didn't deal with abstractions as my colleagues at NYU did; rather, he has a penchant for obtaining first hand evidence. While critics such as Paul Dickson (*The Think Tank*) portrayed Hudson fellows as those unconcerned with the consequences of their studies, I discovered just the reverse. I also discovered there was more openness, a greater willingness to encounter ideas of all kinds, than I had ever observed in my academic career.

However, despite Herman's urging, I decided to remain at the university as a full time scholar; but I continued to maintain an association with Hudson as a visiting associate. I couldn't see myself living in Herman's penumbra. Nonetheless, I became addicted to Herman's methods, particularly his scenario building. Herman would meet with scholars on Wednesday morning to discuss wars in the future. At the time, we were on World War VI. So intrigued was I by his presentations, that I was invariably racing on the Taconic Parkway in an effort to get to the institute on time. Each time, I was stopped by the same patrolman, who would say "speeding again to get to Herman Kahn's lecture." I nodded and took my ticket. In 1970, I held the state record for speeding violations in New York State.

At these no-holds barred events Herman entertained every position, knocking some down, building some up and casting a few aside. Although Herman had been caricatured as a mad scientist intent on social destruction, I observed there was as much reason to attribute social woe to Kahn as there is to blame Einstein for the incineration of Hiroshima. At Hudson science is a process, a way of perceiving natural and social phenomena. It is undeniably a rational process, but one that accounts for chance and possibility. Of course, for the neoromantics, science represents a Faustian lust for dominance. Theodore Roszak, one of those seventies critics, argued science is a justification for "the mad, bad ontology of our culture." It is, to use his pompous phrase, "idolatrous consciousness."

Although it has been argued that technocrats like Herman Kahn do not analyze their assumptions, I found that contention missed the mark by a wide margin. The institute was more exciting, more responsive to different points of view and for more engaged in self-analysis than any academic institution I had encountered. That explained why I jumped at the opportunity to join the institute's board of trustees in 1974. I had emerged from heroin purchaser to trustee in a five year period.

It also marked a turning point in my life. Herman and I became friends. I invited him to offer a course in the Gallatin School I called it "Hermeneutics." Having played the role of Herman's researcher and occasional writer, I was pleased that Herman wrote the introductions for two of my books.

When Herman died in 1983, the future of the institute was problematic. I believed we should move to New York City, but one board member, Dan Quayle, argued that we would be welcomed and supported in Indianapolis by the Lilly Endowment. The blandishments from the Endowment proved irresistible. For twenty years, Hudson—named after The New York river—was placed in the Midwest, a strange disparity between name and location.

In 1997, the board of trustees asked me to take on the responsibility of president. It wasn't easy commuting to Indiana, but I did so, still managing my ties to NYU at the same time. But it was also clear to me that, despite my affection for Indianapolis and its residents, whom I much prefer to those inside the Beltway, the only way to influence public policy decisions is to be in Washington, D.C., or New York. By 2003, the board decided that we should establish Washington, D.C., as our headquarters. This move was personally painful since many in Indianapolis regarded the move as a form of betrayal. It was also obvious to me that maintaining a university position and the presidency of Hudson was not sustainable.

The decision to leave NYU wasn't easy. But there wasn't any comparison between the narrowly conceived and broadly generous positions in the respective institutions. Hudson Institute is a home for the open mind; the university has become a hot house for prejudices. So despite the purple in my blood (the NYU color), I moved on.

What I have subsequently observed is that many young scholars, who would ordinarily covet a position in university life, now believe that working in a think tank is a more desirable career move. How odd that the think tank has come to resemble the university of yesteryear, and the university of today is more akin to the Church of yesteryear—a place for doctrinal study and proselytization.

Conclusion

If my personal odyssey reveals anything it is the dramatic shift that has occurred in this society over the last four decades. Surely detractors will contend that my bias prevents me from seeing events clearly. I would not hesitate to suggest that it is often difficult to generalize from personal experience. All I can say as a defense is that I've tried to be fair. There is more than a dollop of true introspection in the preceding pages.

As Winston Churchill once observed, "We shape a house and then it shapes us." I built, along with my colleagues, a college at NYU and I've helped to rebuild the Hudson Institute from an Indiana-based institution to one based in Washington, D.C. In the process I have been affected.

My observations about what works and doesn't have been called into question many times. I realize, like G. K. Chesterton, that the problem with pragmatism is that it doesn't work. The sensible and the empirical often retreat before the emotional and romantic.

I have also noted that political considerations have entered the Academy as an ideological tsunami. Perhaps these considerations were always there, but certainly not to the same degree. In some ways, it is sad that political concerns, sometimes transmogrified into political correctness, play such an influential role in university affairs. There is no question it has had a chastening affect on debate and discussion, the instruments for social intercourse.

It is unlikely we can recapture Newman's vision of the university or even my rose-colored memory of the Columbia campus, but I remain a guarded optimist. There are colleges like Grove City and Hillsdale that adhere to traditional academic values, and there is promise in on-line universities like Yorktown that adhere to the best that is thought and known. I have also suggested that think tanks are universities in absentia, where some of the brightest students seek refuge from the politicization that affects higher education.

To my surprise, parents are starting to understand the problem as well. Fifty-thousand dollars a year spent on propaganda contending America is a Fascist society and the middle class is comprised of bourgeois pigs seems patently absurd. Many moms and dads are telling Johnnie and Janie that they might be better off getting a job—if they can secure one—and going to college part-time. It is hard of course, to overcome the labeling effect of a college degree from an elite institution, and it is difficult to alter the rite of passage from high school to college. But there are signs that this is happening perhaps precipitated by the economic recession.

Ultimately, societies rise and fall on the cultural principles citizens imbibe. Colleges and universities play a central role in this process. As I see it, the role now being played is often destructive. Instead of a search for truth, there is a desire to transform by following an ideological agenda. For example, there have been mistakes and errors in the American tale. This is, after all, an imperfect nation. But to emphasize the flaws without corresponding mention of achievements to intentionally mislead, is a perversion of the truth. Yet so often American history is anti–American history. And the blemishes are emphasized to the exclusion of accomplishment.

There is also a naïve belief that excellence is elitist, that aspiring to the highest standard is arrogance. The consequence, of course, is that the top quartile is subordinated to the rise of the bottom quartile, creating a compression at the mean or what in common parlance is mediocrity. That universities promote mediocrity is a disgrace and, to make matters worse, it is, in Orwellian terms, often described as excellence.

In this context, I'm reminded of a comment by Charles Eliot, former president at Harvard. Eliot was asked why there is so much intelligence at Harvard. He responded by noting "the freshmen bring so much in and the seniors take so little out." That pungent reply was made many decades ago, but is even more pertinent today.

We have lost our way. But when I look back, I am grateful for the opportunities university life has granted me, a poor boy from Brooklyn with visions of basketball in his imagination. Needless to say, I only hope others can benefit in the same way.

I also have a dream in which universities allow for a free and open exchange of opinion unrestricted by political correctness. I would like to see students eager to learn, who come to recognize the value of reading classic texts. And my experience tells me that only through an adherence to excellence can universities reclaim their ascendant role in society. Of course, I dream because dreams are often the harbinger of change and reform in higher education of the kind I've suggested, is a change I can readily support.

www.ingramcontent.com/pod-product-compliance
Lightning Source LLC
Chambersburg PA
CBHW031555300426
44111CB00006BA/327